D0548805

# Microwave
# FREEZER TO MICROWAVE

**Compiled and Edited by Judith Ferguson**
**Recipes Tested and Prepared by Jacqueline Bellefontaine**
**Photography by Peter Barry**
**Designed by Philip Clucas**
**Produced by Ted Smart, David Gibbon and Gerald Hughes**

CLB 1797
© 1987 Colour Library Books Ltd., Guildford, Surrey, England.
Text filmsetting by Focus Photoset Ltd., London, England.
Printed and bound in Barcelona, Spain by Cronion, S.A.
All rights reserved.
ISBN 0 86283 559 3

**The publishers wish to thank Samsung Electronics (UK) Ltd for the loan of microwave ovens, Corning Ltd for providing Pyrex and microwave cookware dishes and Lakeland Plastics of Windermere, Cumbria for the supply of cookware and accessories.**

# Microwave
# FREEZER TO MICROWAVE

## COOMBE BOOKS

# CONTENTS

Food budgets go much further with a freezer and microwave in the house. Buy food in its season when it's cheapest, and freeze for later use, cooked or uncooked. Either way, defrosting in the microwave is quick and easy. Once you master the principles of freezing and microwave cooking and defrosting you will see what good friends these two appliances can be.

With the defrosting and reheating abilities of a microwave oven menu planning can become crisis-free. Most ovens incorporate an automatic defrosting control in their setting programs. If your oven does not have this facility, use the lowest temperature setting and employ an on/off technique. In other words, turn on for 30 seconds-1 minute and then let the food stand for a minute or two before repeating the process. This procedure allows the food to defrost evenly without starting to cook at the edges.

Always cover the food when defrosting or reheating. Plastic containers, plastic bags and freezer-to-table ware can be used to defrost food in. Meals can be placed on paper or plastic trays and frozen. Cover with cling film/plastic wrap or greaseproof/wax paper. It is usually advisable to defrost food first and then cook or reheat it, but there are exceptions to this rule, so be sure to check instructions on pre-packaged foods before proceeding. Foods frozen in blocks, such as spinach or casseroles, should be broken up as they defrost.

Bread rolls and coffee cakes can be placed on paper plates or covered in paper towels to reheat or defrost. These materials will help protect the food and will absorb the moisture which comes to the surface and could otherwise make the foods soggy. If you want a crisp crust on reheated bread, slip a sheet of foil under the paper towel, and don't cover completely.

When reheating foods in a sauce, stir occasionally to distribute heat evenly. Spread food out in an even layer for uniform heating. Sauces and gravies can be poured over sliced meat and poultry to keep it moist while reheating. To tell if reheating is completed, touch the bottom of the plate or container; if it feels hot, then the food is ready. Foods can be arranged on plates in advance and reheated without over-cooking or drying out, an advantage when entertaining. With a microwave oven you can spend more time with your guests than by yourself in the kitchen!

**All the recipes in this book were prepared in an oven with a 700 watt maximum output. For 500 watt ovens add 40 seconds for each minute stated in the recipe. For 600 watt ovens add 20 seconds for each minute stated in the recipe. If using a 650 watt oven only a slight increase in overall time is necessary.**

Microwave

## FREEZER TO MICROWAVE

# SOUPS

## Potato Soup

**PREPARATION TIME:** 10 minutes

**MICROWAVE COOKING TIME:**
21 minutes

**SERVES:** 4 people

*675g/1½ lbs/4 cups diced potatoes*
*45g/3 tbsps butter or margarine*
*1 onion, thinly sliced*
*280ml/½ pint/1 cup water*
*850ml/1½ pints/3 cups milk*
*30ml/2 tbsps chopped fresh dill or 15ml/*
*    1 tbsp dried dill*
*1 bay leaf*
*Salt and pepper*
*Nutmeg*

**GARNISH**
*Fresh dill*

Put the potatoes, butter and onions
into a large bowl. Cover with cling
film/plastic wrap and pierce several
times. Cook for 10 minutes on
HIGH. Add the milk, water, dill, bay
leaf, seasoning and nutmeg and cook
for 7 minutes on HIGH. Leave to
stand, covered, for 1 minute.
Uncover the soup and allow to cool
slightly. Remove the bay leaf and
pour half the soup into a food
processor or blender and purée until
smooth. Repeat with remaining soup.
Adjust the seasoning and the
consistency and if too thick, add
more milk or water. Allow the soup
to cool and pour into a freezer
container, leaving 2.5cm/1 inch
headspace; seal. Store up to 3
months. To defrost and reheat, cook
on LOW/DEFROST for 12 minutes
in the freezer container without lid.
Transfer the soup to a large bowl and
leave to stand 10 minutes. Cook on
MEDIUM HIGH to HIGH for 10

**This page: Carrot and Orange Soup.
Facing page: Cream of Mushroom
Soup (top) and Potato Soup
(bottom).**

minutes. Break up the soup with a
fork and stir every 5 minutes until
the soup is hot. Serve garnished with
the fresh dill.

## Carrot and Orange Soup

**PREPARATION TIME:** 15 minutes

**MICROWAVE COOKING TIME:**
24 minutes

**SERVES:** 4 people

*180g/6oz/1 cup chopped carrots*
*1 onion, peeled and finely chopped*

## Red Pepper Soup

**PREPARATION TIME:** 15 minutes

**MICROWAVE COOKING TIME:** 15 minutes

**SERVES:** 4 people

*3 red peppers, seeded and chopped*
*3 tomatoes, seeded and roughly chopped*
*1 medium onion, peeled and finely chopped*
*1150ml/2 pints/4 cups chicken or vegetable stock*
*30ml/2 tbsps cornflour/cornstarch*
*Salt and pepper*

**GARNISH** *(after defrosting)*
*½ red pepper, finely chopped*
*Chopped parsley*

Place the peppers, tomatoes and onions in a large bowl with the stock, salt and pepper. Stir in the cornflour/cornstarch. Loosely cover and cook on HIGH for 15 minutes, stirring often. Allow the soup to stand for 1-2 minutes and then purée in a food processor or blender. Allow the soup to cool completely and pour into a freezer container. Seal well and freeze up to 3 months. To defrost and reheat, follow the directions for Tomato and Basil Soup. When the soup has defrosted completely, reheat for 2-3 minutes on HIGH with the diced red pepper garnish. Sprinkle with chopped parsley just before serving.

## Winter Vegetable Soup

**PREPARATION TIME:** 25 minutes

**MICROWAVE COOKING TIME:** 15 minutes

**SERVES:** 4-6 people

*1 litre/1¾ pints/3½ cups vegetable stock*
*1 potato, peeled and diced*
*½ small swede/rutabaga, peeled and diced*
*1-2 turnips, depending upon size, peeled and diced*

*350g/12oz/2 cups diced potatoes*
*850ml/1½ pints/3 cups vegetable or chicken stock*
*45g/3 tbsps butter or margarine*
*280ml/½ pint/1 cup milk*
*1 orange*
*5ml/1 tsp ground ginger*
*Pinch sugar*
*Salt and pepper*

Combine the carrots, potatoes and onion in a large, deep bowl. Cover loosely and cook for 10 minutes on HIGH. Add the stock, milk, ginger and the juice of the orange, reserving the peel. Add a pinch of sugar, salt and pepper and re-cover the bowl. Cook for further 10 minutes on HIGH. Leave to stand, covered, for 1 minute. Meanwhile, scrape the white pith from the orange peel and cut the peel into short, thin strips. Put into a small bowl and just cover with water. Cook on HIGH for 2 minutes to soften the peel. Drain and rinse in cold water and set aside. Uncover the soup and allow to cool slightly. Pour half the soup into a food processor or blender and purée until smooth. Repeat with remaining soup. Mix in reserved orange peel strips and pour the soup into a freezer container. Allow to cool, seal and store for up to 3 months. To defrost and reheat, follow the instructions for Potato Soup. The soup may also be served chilled. If desired, serve garnished with a swirl of cream.

**This page: Red Pepper Soup. Facing page: Winter Vegetable Soup (top) and Hot and Sour Soup (bottom).**

1 carrot, peeled and diced
½ small head white cabbage, shredded
1 leek, thinly sliced and well washed
1 bouquet garni (1 bay leaf, 1 sprig thyme,
   3 parsley stalks)
10ml/2 tsps tomato purée/paste
   (optional)
Salt and pepper
30ml/2 tbsps chopped parsley

Combine the stock, bouquet garni, potato, swede/rutabaga, turnips and carrots in a large, deep bowl. Loosely cover and cook for 10 minutes on HIGH. Add the cabbage and leeks and cook a further 5 minutes on HIGH. Add the tomato purée/paste, if using, salt and pepper. Allow the soup to cool completely and remove the bouquet garni. Pour the soup into a freezer container, leaving 2.5cm/1 inch headspace on top. Seal and freeze for up to 3 months. To defrost and reheat, cook for 10 minutes on DEFROST and stand 10 minutes, stirring occasionally to help break-up the soup. Do not over-stir; the vegetables should remain whole. When the stock and the vegetables have defrosted, pour the soup into a bowl or serving dish and reheat on HIGH for 4-5 minutes before serving. Add the chopped parsley just before serving and adjust the seasoning.

## Parsnip and Carrot Soup

**PREPARATION TIME:** 10 minutes

**MICROWAVE COOKING TIME:**
10 minutes

**SERVES:** 4 people

225g/8oz parsnips, peeled and finely
   chopped or grated
225g/8oz carrots, peeled and finely
   chopped or grated
280ml/½ pint/1 cup stock or water
570ml/1 pint/2 cups milk
Pinch ground nutmeg
Salt and pepper
1 small bunch chives, snipped
60-140ml/2-5oz single/light cream

Place the parsnips, carrots, water, salt and pepper and nutmeg into a large, deep bowl. Cover and cook on HIGH for 10 minutes, stirring

occasionally. Add the milk and leave the soup to stand for 1 minute. Uncover and allow to cool slightly. Pour the soup into a blender or food processor and purée until smooth. Add the chives and allow the soup to cool completely. Pour into a freezer container, seal and store for up to 3 months. To defrost and reheat, follow the instructions for Potato Soup. Just before serving, stir in the cream.

## Cream of Mushroom Soup

**PREPARATION TIME:** 10 minutes

**MICROWAVE COOKING TIME:**
17 minutes

**SERVES:** 4 people

340g/12oz mushrooms, cleaned and
   finely chopped
1 shallot, finely chopped
30g/2 tbsps butter or margarine
45g/3 tbsps plain/all-purpose flour
1 sprig rosemary
570ml/1 pint/2 cups chicken or
   vegetable stock
430ml/¾ pint/1½ cups milk
Salt and pepper
Pinch nutmeg
30ml/2 tbsps dry sherry
90ml/3 fl oz/⅓ cup double/heavy cream

Put the mushrooms, shallot and butter into a large glass bowl. Cover loosely and cook on HIGH for 4 minutes, or until the mushrooms are soft. Stir occasionally. Add the flour and stir in well. Add the sprig of rosemary and gradually add the stock and milk. Add salt, pepper and nutmeg and re-cover the bowl. Cook a further 6 minutes on HIGH, or until boiling. Stir several times during cooking. Allow the soup to stand for 1-2 minutes, covered. Purée the soup in a food processor or blender, if desired, in 2 batches. Allow the soup to cool completely and then pour into a freezer container. Freeze for up to 3 months. To defrost and reheat, follow the instructions for Potato Soup. Just before reheating, stir in the sherry and the double/heavy cream. Adjust the seasoning and serve.

## Split Pea Soup with Bacon

**PREPARATION TIME:** 15 minutes

**MICROWAVE COOKING TIME:**
40 minutes-1¼ hours

**SERVES:** 4 people

4 slices bacon/streaky bacon, bones and
   rind removed
2 shallots, finely chopped
1700ml/3 pints/6 cups hot water
225g/8oz/1 cup dried green split peas
2 small carrots, thinly sliced
5ml/1 tsp chopped thyme
15ml/1 tbsp chopped parsley
1 bay leaf
430-850ml/¾-1½ pints/1½-3 cups
   vegetable stock
Salt and pepper
Dash Worcestershire sauce

Combine the bacon and the shallots in a large, deep bowl. Cover with paper towels and cook on HIGH for 2-3 minutes, or until the bacon is brown. Add the remaining ingredients and cover the bowl loosely. Cook on HIGH for 40 minutes-1¼ hours, or until the peas are soft, stirring every 10 minutes. Remove the bay leaf and allow the soup to cool completely. Purée in a food processor and add stock to bring soup to the consistency of unwhipped cream. Pour the soup into a freezer container, leaving 2.5cm/1 inch headspace. Seal well and freeze for up to 3 months. To defrost and reheat, follow instructions for Potato Soup. Garnish with fresh chopped parsley before serving, if desired.

## Hot and Sour Soup

**PREPARATION TIME:** 15 minutes

**MICROWAVE COOKING TIME:**
18-20 minutes

**SERVES:** 4 people

1 chicken breast
1150ml/2 pints/4 cups hot water
2 carrots, thinly sliced on the diagonal

**Facing page: Parsnip and Carrot Soup (top) and Split Pea Soup with Bacon (bottom).**

*2 sticks celery, cut in thin diagonal slices*
*120g/4oz sliced mushrooms*
*30ml/2 tbsps cornflour/cornstarch*
*30ml/2 tbsps white wine or rice vinegar*
*15ml/1 tbsp soy sauce*
*Dash sesame oil and tabasco*
*1 egg, slightly beaten*

Combine the chicken, water, carrot and celery in a large, deep bowl. Cover loosely and cook on HIGH 8-10 minutes, or until the chicken is no longer pink. Turn the meat over and stir the ingredients from time to time. Remove the chicken and vegetables and reserve the stock. Allow the chicken to cool and remove the skin and bones. Cut the chicken into thin shreds. Add the chicken and mushrooms to the stock and cook a further 4-6 minutes on HIGH. Mix the cornflour/cornstarch, vinegar, soy sauce, sesame oil and tabasco, and stir into the stock. Cook on HIGH 1-2 minutes, or until slightly thickened. Allow the soup to cool completely and combine with the reserved carrot and celery. Pour into a freezer container and cover well. Be sure to leave 2.5cm/1 inch headspace in the container before sealing. Store for up to 3 months. To defrost and reheat, follow the instructions for Winter Vegetable Soup. When soup is piping hot, pour in the beaten egg in a thin stream, stirring constantly.

## Tomato and Basil Soup

**PREPARATION TIME:** 10 minutes

**MICROWAVE COOKING TIME:**
20-25 minutes

**SERVES:** 4 people

*800g (2 8oz cans tomatoes)*
*2 onions, finely chopped*
*570ml/1 pint/2 cups beef or chicken*
*    stock*
*15ml/1 tbsp tomato purée/paste*
*30ml/2 tbsps chopped basil*
*Pinch ground allspice*
*1 bay leaf*
*Pinch sugar*
*Salt and pepper*
*60ml/4 tbsps red wine*
*30ml/2 tbsps cornflour/cornstarch*

**GARNISH** *(after defrosting)*
*Fresh basil leaves*

Put the tomatoes and their juice, onions, stock, tomato purée/paste, basil, allspice and salt and pepper into a large bowl. Cook, uncovered, for 12-15 minutes on HIGH, stirring occasionally. Add a pinch of sugar if necessary, to bring out the tomato flavour. Sieve the tomatoes, extracting as much pulp as possible. Add basil and blend the wine and cornflour/cornstarch and stir into the soup. Cook, uncovered, for 8-10 minutes on HIGH, stirring often until thickened. Allow the soup to cool completely and pour into a freezer container, leaving 2.5cm/1 inch headspace. Seal well and store

for up to 3 months. To defrost and reheat, warm for 10 minutes on DEFROST. Stand for 10 minutes, breaking-up the soup with a fork as it defrosts. When completely melted, pour the soup into a serving dish and reheat 4-5 minutes on HIGH, or until hot. Garnish with fresh basil leaves before serving.

## Italian Onion Soup

**PREPARATION TIME:** 10 minutes

**MICROWAVE COOKING TIME:**
22-33 minutes

**SERVES:** 4-6 people

*675g/1½ lbs onions, thinly sliced*

*450g/16oz can plum tomatoes*
*30g/2 tbsps butter or margarine*
*30g/2 tbsps plain/all-purpose flour*
*140ml/¼ pint/½ cup red wine*
*570ml/1 pint/2 cups beef stock*
*1.25ml/¼ tsp basil*
*1.25ml/¼ tsp oregano*
*Tomato purée/paste*
*1 bay leaf*
*Salt and pepper*

**GARNISH** *(after defrosting)*
*4 slices French bread, toasted and*
   *buttered*
*60g/2 tbsps Mozzarella cheese, grated*
*60g/2 tbsps Parmesan cheese, grated*

Place the onions and butter in a large bowl and loosely cover. Cook on HIGH for 12-16 minutes, stirring occasionally. Stir in the flour and add the tomatoes and their juice, wine, stock, basil, oregano and bay leaf. Add a pinch of salt and pepper and re-cover the bowl. Cook on HIGH for 8 minutes, stirring occasionally. Reduce the setting to LOW and cook a further 4 minutes. Leave to stand, covered, for 1-2 minutes. Adjust the seasoning and add enough tomato purée/paste to give a good tomato colour and flavour. Allow the

soup to cool completely and remove the bay leaf. Pour the soup into a freezer container, leaving 2.5cm/ 1 inch headspace. Seal well and freeze for up to 3 months. Defrost and reheat as for French Onion Soup. Combine the cheeses and sprinkle onto the slices of toasted French bread. Place on a plate and cook on LOW until the cheese starts to melt. Grill/broil conventionally until lightly browned, and place on top of the hot soup to serve.

## French Onion Soup

| | |
|---|---|
| **PREPARATION TIME:** 10 minutes | |
| **MICROWAVE COOKING TIME:** 30-34 minutes | |
| **SERVES:** 4-6 people | |

*675g/1½ lbs onions, thinly sliced*
*30g/2 tbsps butter or margarine*
*30g/2 tbsps plain/all-purpose flour*
*140ml/¼ pint/½ cup dry cider or white*
   *wine*
*1150ml/2 pints/4 cups beef stock*
*1.25ml/¼ tsp thyme*
*1 bay leaf*
*Salt and pepper*
*30ml/2 tbsps brandy*

**Facing page: Italian Onion Soup (top) and French Onion Soup (bottom). Above left: Tomato and Basil Soup. Above right: Creamy Spinach Soup.**

**GARNISH** *(after defrosting)*
*4 slices French bread, toasted and*
   *buttered*
*60g/2oz/½ cup Gruyere or Swiss cheese*

Place the onions and the butter in a large bowl and loosely cover. Cook on HIGH for 12-16 minutes, stirring occasionally. Stir in the flour and add the wine or cider, stock, thyme, bay leaf, salt and pepper. Re-cover the bowl and cook on HIGH for 10 minutes. Stir occasionally. Reduce the setting to LOW and cook a further 8 minutes. Leave the bowl to stand, covered, for 1-2 minutes. Remove the bay leaf and allow the soup to cool completely. Pour into a freezer container, leaving 1 inch headspace. Seal well and freeze for up to 3 months. To defrost and reheat, warm for 10 minutes on LOW or DEFROST and stand 10 minutes, breaking the soup up occasionally with a fork, but taking care not to break-up the onions. Once the soup has completely defrosted, add brandy, pour into a serving dish and reheat for 4-5 minutes on HIGH. Top the bread with the grated cheese and place on a plate. Cook on LOW until the cheese begins to melt and then grill/broil conventionally until lightly browned. Top the soup with the cheese toast and serve immediately.

## Creamy Spinach Soup

**PREPARATION TIME:** 15 minutes

**MICROWAVE COOKING TIME:** 21 minutes

**SERVES:** 4-6 people

900g/2lbs fresh spinach, washed
   and stems removed
30g/2 tbsps butter or margarine
1 shallot, finely chopped
30g/2 tbsps plain/all-purpose flour
700ml/1¼ pints/1½ cups chicken or
   vegetable stock
1.25ml/¼ tsp marjoram
Squeeze lemon juice
Grated nutmeg
Salt and pepper
430ml/¾ pint/1½ cups milk
140ml/¼ pint/½ cup cream
1 bay leaf

**GARNISH** (after defrosting)
Thinly sliced lemon or 1 hard-boiled egg,
   chopped

Put the washed spinach into a roasting bag and tie loosely. Stand the bag upright in the oven and cook for 5 minutes on HIGH, or until the spinach is just wilted. Turn bag once. Put the butter and shallot into a large bowl, cover and cook for 5 minutes on HIGH. Stir in the flour and cook a further 2 minutes on HIGH. Add the stock, marjoram, bay leaf and grated nutmeg. Cook for 2 minutes on HIGH, stirring occasionally, until thickened. Add the spinach, salt, pepper and lemon juice and cook for 3 minutes on HIGH. Stir the milk into the soup and pour the soup into a food processor or blender and purée in 2 batches until smooth. Allow the soup to cool completely

and pour into a freezer container. Seal and freeze for up to 3 months. To defrost and reheat, follow the instructions for Potato Soup. Before serving, add the cream and adjust the seasoning. Serve garnished with thin slices of lemon or chopped hard-boiled egg.

## Salad Soup

**PREPARATION TIME:** 10 minutes

**MICROWAVE COOKING TIME:** 20 minutes

**SERVES:** 4-6 people

2-3 potatoes, peeled and diced
6 spring/green onions, finely chopped
½ head lettuce, shredded
120g/4oz fresh spinach leaves, washed
   and stems removed
1 small bunch watercress, well washed
   and thick stems removed
½ cucumber, peeled and grated
30ml/2 tbsps chopped parsley
430-570ml/¾-1 pint/1½-2 cups chicken
   or vegetable stock
570ml/1 pint/2 cups milk
Pinch nutmeg
Pinch cayenne pepper
Salt and pepper
140ml/¼ pint/½ cup single/light cream

**GARNISH** (after defrosting)
Natural yogurt
Chopped parsley

Put the potatoes into a large bowl and cover loosely. Cook for 7 minutes on HIGH, stirring occasionally. Add the vegetables, herbs and stock to the potatoes and re-cover the bowl. Cook for further 5 minutes on HIGH. Stir in the milk and add the nutmeg, cayenne pepper, salt, pepper and cream. Leave the soup to stand, covered, for 1-2 minutes and then pour into a blender or food processor. Purée the soup until smooth, and allow to cool completely. Pour into a freezer container, leaving at least 2.5cm/ 1 inch headspace. Seal well and freeze for up to 3 months. To defrost and reheat, follow the instructions for Potato Soup. Serve garnished with spoonfuls of natural yogurt sprinkled with chopped parsley.

## Broad/Lima Bean and Ham Soup with Mint

**PREPARATION TIME:** 15 minutes

**MICROWAVE COOKING TIME:** 10 minutes

**SERVES:** 4-6 people

30g/2oz butter or margarine
2 onions, finely chopped
15ml/1 tbsp plain/all-purpose flour
1150ml/2 pints/4 cups chicken or
   vegetable stock
140g/1lb frozen broad/lima beans
1 bouquet garni (1 bay leaf, 1 sprig thyme,
   3 parsley stalks)
225g/8oz cooked ham, cut into small
   cubes
15ml/1 tbsp chopped mint
15ml/1 tbsp chopped parsley
2 egg yolks
140ml/¼ pint/½ cup double/heavy
   cream
Salt and pepper

**GARNISH** (after defrosting)
Fresh mint leaves

Place the butter and the onions in a large, deep bowl and cook for 2 minutes on HIGH, loosely covered, to soften the onions. Stir in the flour and gradually add the stock. Add the beans, bouquet garni, chopped mint, chopped parsley and salt and pepper. Re-cover the bowl and cook a further 10 minutes on HIGH, or until the beans are very tender. Remove the bouquet garni and allow the soup to cool slightly. Purée in a food processor or blender in 2 batches until smooth and sieve if desired. Add the ham to the soup and allow the soup to cool completely. Pour into a freezer container, leaving 2.5cm/1 inch headspace. Seal and freeze for up to 3 months. Defrost and reheat as for Potato Soup. Serve garnished with whole fresh mint leaves.

**Facing page: Salad Soup** (top) and **Broad/Lima Bean and Ham Soup with Mint** (bottom).

*Microwave*

# FREEZER TO MICROWAVE

# APPETIZERS

## Chicken Liver Pâté

**PREPARATION TIME:** 8 minutes

**MICROWAVE COOKING TIME:** 9 minutes

**SERVES:** 4 people

450g/1lb chicken livers
1 shallot, finely chopped
1 clove garlic, crushed
1 large sprig rosemary
45g/3 tbsps butter
15ml/1 tbsp parsley
15ml/1 tbsp Madeira or sherry
15ml/1 tbsp cream
Nutmeg
Salt and pepper

**GARNISH** (after defrosting)
Juniper berries
Small sprigs rosemary

Pick over the livers, removing any discoloured parts. Put the livers, shallot, garlic, rosemary and half the butter into a bowl. Cover with pierced cling film/plastic wrap and cook for 6 minutes on HIGH, stirring once. Remove the rosemary and put the mixture into a food processor with the Madeira and parsley. Purée until smooth and stir in the cream. Allow the mixture to cool and then add the remaining butter. Purée again to mix well. Divide the pâté between 4 small dishes and allow to cool completely. Cover well and freeze for up to 2 months. To defrost and serve, warm the pâté on DEFROST for about 2 minutes. Turn and rearrange the dishes often, taking care that the edges of the pâté do not heat up. Allow the pâté to stand for at least 20 minutes before serving to complete the defrosting process. Garnish with fresh rosemary and juniper berries.

## Kipper Pâté

**PREPARATION TIME:** 10 minutes

**MICROWAVE COOKING TIME:** 2½-3½ minutes

**SERVES:** 4 people

225g/8oz kipper fillets
60g/4 tbsps butter or margarine
45ml/3 tbsps double/heavy cream

This page: **Mushrooms à la Grecque.** Facing page: **Kipper Pâté (top) and Chicken Liver Pâté (bottom).**

15ml/1 tbsp lemon juice
5ml/1 tsp grated horseradish or
   horseradish sauce
Pinch salt
Coarsely ground black pepper

**GARNISH** (*after defrosting*)
*Lemon slices*

Place the kippers in a small, shallow dish and cover loosely. Cook on HIGH for 2-3 minutes or until the fish breaks easily. Remove the skin and any bones and set the fish aside. Melt the butter for 30 seconds on HIGH in a deep bowl. Combine the butter and kippers in a food processor and purée until smooth. Add the lemon juice, cream and horseradish sauce and work until blended. Taste and add salt, if desired, and stir in the coarsely-ground black pepper by hand. Divide the mixture among 4 serving dishes and smooth the top. Alternatively, freeze in 1 container. Allow to cool completely before freezing and cover well. May be kept for up to 1 month. To defrost before serving, heat for 2 minutes on LOW or DEFROST, making sure the mixture does not begin to heat up. Leave to stand for 10 minutes to complete the defrosting. Serve garnished with lemon slices and hot or melba toast.

## Pinwheels

**PREPARATION TIME:** 20 minutes

**MICROWAVE COOKING TIME:** 3½-6½ minutes

**SERVES:** 6-8 people

*180g/6oz ham, finely chopped*
*30ml/2 tbsps garlic and herb soft cheese*
*30ml/2 tbsps prepared mayonnaise*
*6 black olives, pitted and chopped*
*30g/2 tbsps chopped pecans or walnuts*
*6 slices whole-wheat bread*
*60g/4 tbsps butter or margarine*
*1 egg*
*60g/4 tbsps sesame seeds*

Mix the ham, cheese, mayonnaise, olives and nuts and set aside. Trim the crusts from the bread and roll each slice of bread until very thin. Spread each slice with the ham mixture and roll up as for a Swiss roll/jelly roll. Melt the butter in a shallow dish for 30-45 seconds on HIGH. Beat the egg lightly and slowly beat into the butter. Coat the rolls in the butter and egg mixture and then roll in the sesame seeds to coat thoroughly. Chill to firm and then wrap each roll individually and freeze for up to 2 weeks. To serve, unwrap the rolls and slice each into 6 pieces with a sharp knife. Place the slices in circles on two plates. Microwave each plate on HIGH for 3-6 minutes or until the pinwheel slices are hot. Turn the plate once or twice during cooking.

## Mushrooms à la Grecque

**PREPARATION TIME:** 15 minutes

**MICROWAVE COOKING TIME:** 10 minutes

**SERVES:** 4 people

*450g/1 lb mushrooms, quartered if large*
*30g/2 tbsps butter or margarine*
*120g/4oz canned plum tomatoes, drained and broken up*
*2.5ml/½ tsp coriander seeds, slightly crushed*
*2.5ml/½ tsp cumin seeds, slightly crushed*
*2.5ml/½ tsp fennel seeds, slightly crushed*
*30ml/2 tbsps tomato purée/paste*
*Juice of half lemon*
*15ml/1 tbsp chopped parsley*
*10ml/2 tsps chopped fresh coriander leaves*
*1 clove garlic, crushed*
*2 shallots, finely chopped*
*Salt and pepper*
*30g/2 tbsps cornflour/cornstarch*

*45ml/3 tbsps dry white wine*
*Salt and pepper*

Place the mushrooms and butter in a large, deep bowl. Cook on HIGH for 5 minutes. Stir in the remaining ingredients except for the wine and cornflour/cornstarch. Cook a further 2 minutes on HIGH, loosely covered. Take some of the hot sauce and pour into the cornflour/cornstarch and white wine mixture and return it to the bowl. Stir well and cook a further 3 minutes on HIGH until the cornflour/cornstarch thickens. Allow to cool completely and divide among individual serving dishes or a large freezer container. Cover well and freeze for up to 3 weeks. To defrost, cook gently on DEFROST or LOW for 10 minutes, breaking up occasionally with a fork, but being careful not to break up the mushrooms. Leave to stand 10 minutes. May be served hot or cold with toast or pitta bread.

## Gnocchi Verde

**PREPARATION TIME:** 20 minutes

**MICROWAVE COOKING TIME:** 10-13 minutes

**SERVES:** 6-8 people

*675g/1½ lbs fresh spinach, well washed*
  *and stalks removed, or 300g/10oz*
  *frozen, chopped spinach*
*340g/12oz/¾ cup Fontina or Gruyere*
  *cheese, finely grated*
*30g/2 tbsps Parmesan cheese, grated*
*1 clove garlic, crushed*
*60g/2oz/½ cup fresh white breadcrumbs*
*1.25ml/¼ tsp oregano*
*Salt and pepper*
*Pinch nutmeg*
*1 egg, beaten*

Cook the spinach in a roasting bag or loosely covered bowl for 4-5 minutes on HIGH, or until wilted. Alternatively, cook the frozen spinach 4-5 minutes on HIGH, or until defrosted. Drain the spinach well, pressing out any excess liquid. Add all the remaining ingredients, adding the egg gradually to bind the mixture together. Shape the mixture into 2.5cm/1 inch balls. Place on a

**Facing page: Pinwheels (top) and Gnocchi Verde (bottom). This page: Pork and Peppercorn Pâté.**

plate lined with wax/greaseproof paper and cover loosely. Freeze until firm and then pack in a container. Keep in the freezer for up to 2 weeks. To serve, place the balls well apart on a plate or microwave-proof baking sheet. Cook from frozen for 2 minutes on HIGH. Reduce the power to MEDIUM and cook for further 4-6 minutes, re-arranging once or twice. Serve hot.

## Pork and Peppercorn Pâté

**PREPARATION TIME:** 10 minutes

**MICROWAVE COOKING TIME:** 15 minutes

**SERVES:** 6-8 people

*225g/8oz minced/ground pork*
*225g/8oz minced/ground veal*
*120g/4oz ham, minced*
*120g/4oz pig/pork liver*
*90g/3oz minced/ground pork fat*
*1 clove garlic, crushed*
*60ml/4 tbsps brandy*
*Ground allspice*
*1.25ml/¼ tsp thyme*
*10ml/2 tsps green peppercorns*
*10ml/2 tsps pink peppercorns*

225g/8oz sliced bacon/smoked streaky
    bacon
Salt and pepper

Remove skin and ducts from the liver
and chop in a food processor once or
twice. Add the minced/ground
meats, ham, pork fat, garlic, brandy,
allspice and thyme. Process to blend
but do not over-work. Stir in the
peppercorns by hand. Line a loaf dish
with the strips of bacon and press in
the pâté mixture on top. Fold any
overlapping strips of bacon over the
top of the pâté and cover it well.
Cook on MEDIUM for 6 minutes and
then leave to stand for 5
minutes. Cook a further 10 minutes
on MEDIUM. Cover with foil, press
down and weight. Leave to stand for
2 hours to firm up and then store in
the freezer for up to 1 month. Defrost
as for Pâté aux Herbes. Serve sliced
with salad and French bread.

**This page: Fennel Provençale.
Facing page: Coquilles au Poisson
Fumé (top) and Sweet and Sour
Cocktail Meatballs (bottom).**

## Fennel Provençale

**PREPARATION TIME:** 20 minutes

**MICROWAVE COOKING TIME:**
16-20 minutes

**SERVES:** 4 people

4 small bulbs fennel

**SAUCE**
225g/8oz canned plum tomatoes
1 clove garlic, crushed
2 shallots, finely chopped
15ml/1 tbsp capers
15ml/1 tbsp chopped black olives
10ml/2 tsps chopped basil
15ml/1 tbsp chopped parsley

Pinch sugar
Salt and pepper
60ml/4 tbsps dry white wine
30ml/2 tbsps cornflour/cornstarch
60ml/4 tbsps Gruyere cheese, grated
Dry breadcrumbs

Barely trim the ends of the fennel
and cut the bulbs in half, lengthwise.
Remove the core and place the bulbs
in a shallow dish with 60ml/4 tbsps
water. Cover loosely and cook 6-10
minutes on HIGH or until just
tender. Remove from from the
cooking liquid and allow to cool.
Combine all the sauce ingredients in
a glass measure or a small, deep bowl.
Cook on HIGH for 5 minutes,
stirring once or twice until thickened.
Place 2 fennel halves in each of 4
serving dishes. Spoon over the sauce,
leaving some of the fennel showing.
Sprinkle with cheese and then lightly
sprinkle with breadcrumbs. Allow to
cool completely and cover each dish
well. Alternatively, arrange in 1 serving
dish. Freeze for up to 1 month. To
defrost, heat on LOW or DEFROST
for 5 minutes. Leave to stand for 5-10
minutes to complete the defrosting.
To reheat, cook for 5 minutes on
HIGH, and brown under a grill/
broiler before serving if desired.

## Coquilles au Poisson Fumé

**PREPARATION TIME:** 15 minutes

**MICROWAVE COOKING TIME:**
12 minutes

**SERVES:** 4 people

675g/1½ lbs smoked haddock or cod
280ml/½ pint/1¼ cups milk
1 bay leaf
6 black peppercorns
15ml/1 tbsp butter or margarine
1 shallot, finely chopped
120g/4oz small mushrooms, quartered or
    sliced
30g/2 tbsps cornflour/cornstarch
60ml/4 tbsps dry white wine
1 pimento cap, chopped

**TOPPING**
60g/4 tbsps dry breadcrumbs
60g/4 tbsps Parmesan cheese
30g/2 tbsps butter
Paprika

Place the fish and half the milk in a shallow dish. Add the bay leaf and peppercorns and cover loosely. Cook on HIGH for 2 minutes and set aside to cool in the liquid. Skin the fish and remove any bones. Flake the fish and set it aside. Reserve the cooking liquid from the fish. Melt the butter or margarine in a small, deep bowl and add the shallot and mushrooms. Cook for 5 minutes on HIGH. Strain on the cooking liquid from the fish and add the remaining milk. Mix the cornflour/cornstarch with the wine and stir into the sauce. Cook a further 5 minutes on HIGH, stirring occasionally until thickened. Stir in the chopped pimento and the reserved flaked fish. Divide the mixture between 4 small dishes and smooth the top. Melt the remaining butter and mix together the breadcrumbs and the Parmesan cheese. Sprinkle on top of each dish and drizzle over the melted butter. Sprinkle lightly with paprika and allow to cool completely. Cover well and freeze for up to 1 month. To defrost, cook for 7 minutes on DEFROST or LOW and allow 5 minutes standing time. Reheat on HIGH for 3 minutes and brown under a grill/broiler if desired before serving.

## Stuffed Courgettes/ Zucchini

**PREPARATION TIME:** 10 minutes

**MICROWAVE COOKING TIME:** 18 minutes

**SERVES:** 4 people

4 even-sized courgettes/zucchini
15ml/1 tbsp butter or margarine
1 shallot, finely chopped
280ml/½ pint/1 cup milk
30g/2 tbsps cornflour/cornstarch
16 pimento-stuffed olives, roughly chopped
15ml/1 tbsp chopped parsley
2.5ml/½ tsp chopped basil

**TOPPING**
60g/4 tbsps dry breadcrumbs
60g/4 tbsps Parmesan cheese, grated
30g/2 tbsps butter
Salt and pepper

**GARNISH** (after defrosting)
Stuffed olives
Fresh basil leaves

Trim the ends of the courgettes/ zucchini and cut them in half, lengthwise. Place in a large, shallow dish with 60ml/4 tbsps water. Cover loosely with cling film/plastic wrap and cook for 4-5 minutes on HIGH. Rinse in cold water until completely cooled and drain. Carefully scoop out the flesh with a teaspoon, leaving a thin lining of flesh inside the skin. Meanwhile, melt the butter in a small, deep bowl and cook the shallot to soften. Reserve 60ml/4 tbsps of milk and add the rest to the shallot. Combine the milk with the cornflour/cornstarch and add to the bowl. Cook until thickened, about 2-3 minutes on HIGH, stirring once or twice. Add the chopped herbs and the olives. Add the chopped flesh from the courgettes/zucchini to the sauce mixture and stir well. Add salt and pepper to taste and fill the courgette/zucchini shells with the mixture. Sprinkle over the mixture of dry breadcrumbs and Parmesan cheese and melt the remaining butter for 30 seconds on HIGH. Drizzle over the courgettes/zucchini and place them in a serving dish. Cover well and freeze for up to 1 month. To defrost, heat on LOW or DEFROST for about 4 minutes. Leave to stand approximately 5 minutes and then reheat on HIGH for 3-5 minutes or until piping hot. Grill/broil if desired before serving. Garnish with olives and basil.

## Sweet and Sour Cocktail Meatballs

**PREPARATION TIME:** 25 minutes

**MICROWAVE COOKING TIME:** 7-11 minutes

**SERVES:** 4-6 people

225g/8oz minced/ground pork or beef
1 clove garlic, minced
60g/2oz unblanched almonds, finely chopped
Salt and pepper

**SAUCE**
225g/8oz canned pineapple pieces/ chunks, drained and 90ml/3 fl oz/ ⅓ cup juice reserved
15ml/1 tbsp brown sugar
10ml/2 tsps cornflour/cornstarch
1.25ml/¼ tsp ground ginger
15ml/1 tbsp white wine vinegar
15ml/1 tbsp soy sauce
15ml/1 tbsp tomato ketchup

Combine the meatball mixture and shape into 2.5cm/1 inch balls. Place in a circle on a plate or shallow baking dish and cook for 4 minutes, or until the meatballs are firm and no longer pink. Rearrange the meatballs once during cooking. Set the pineapple chunks aside while mixing together the sauce ingredients. Cook the sauce in a glass measure or a deep bowl for 3-7 minutes on HIGH, or until thickened. Combine the sauce with the pineapple and the meatballs and stir carefully. Allow to cool completely and arrange in a serving dish. Cover tightly and freeze for up to 1 month. To defrost, cook on LOW or DEFROST for about 4 minutes, stirring the mixture as it defrosts. Leave to stand for 5 minutes and repeat until completely defrosted. Cook a further 6 minutes on HIGH, stirring once or twice.

## Chicken and Tongue Rolls

**PREPARATION TIME:** 15 minutes

**MICROWAVE COOKING TIME:** 10 minutes

**SERVES:** 4 people

4 chicken legs
4 slices smoked tongue
30ml/2 tbsps grated Parmesan cheese
15ml/1 tbsp grated Gruyere or Cheddar cheese
15ml/1 tbsp chopped parsley
15ml/1 tbsp white wine
Salt and pepper

Remove the bones from the chicken legs and flatten them out. Divide the tongue equally between each chicken

**Facing page: Stuffed Courgettes/ Zucchini.**

leg. Mix together with the grated cheeses, parsley and salt and pepper. Place a spoonful of the mixture on top of each piece of tongue. Roll-up the chicken and tie the rolls with string two or three times. Place the rolls in a shallow dish with the white wine and partially cover. Cook the rolls on HIGH for 5 minutes. Turn over once during cooking and cook a further 5 minutes on HIGH. Allow the rolls to cool, covered, in the cooking liquid. When cool, remove the string and cover tightly. Freeze for up to 1 month. To defrost, use either LOW or DEFROST and heat for 5 minutes. Leave to stand for 5 minutes and repeat the process until completely defrosted. Reheat 4-5 minutes on HIGH if desired. Slice each roll into rounds and serve hot or cold, garnished with parsley and tomatoes if desired.

## Stuffed Mushrooms

**PREPARATION TIME:** 8 minutes

**MICROWAVE COOKING TIME:**
6-8 minutes

**SERVES:** 6 people

*6 large or 12 small mushrooms*
*120g/4oz ham, finely chopped*
*60g/2oz/½ cup fresh white breadcrumbs*
*75g/6 tbsps finely chopped walnuts*
*1 egg, beaten*
*1 bunch chives, snipped*
*15ml/1 tbsp chopped parsley*
*15ml/1 tbsp Dijon mustard*
*Dry breadcrumbs*
*45g/3 tbsps butter*
*Salt and pepper*

Clean the mushrooms, trimming the stalks and chopping them finely. Mix the mushroom stalks with the ham, white breadcrumbs, walnuts, herbs, mustard and seasoning. Gradually beat in the egg to bind together. Pile the mixture on top of the mushrooms and set them aside. Melt the butter for 30 seconds on HIGH and set aside to cool slightly. Sprinkle the dry breadcrumbs on top of the mushrooms and drizzle over the melted butter. Place on a plate and freeze in one layer. Cover well and keep in the freezer for up to 1 month.

To defrost, cook on LOW or DEFROST for about 4 minutes, rotating the mushrooms occasionally. To reheat, increase the setting to HIGH and cook for about 5 minutes. The mushrooms may be browned under a grill/broiler just before serving.

## Pâté aux Herbes

**PREPARATION TIME:** 20 minutes

**MICROWAVE COOKING TIME:**
20 minutes

**SERVES:** 4 people

*300g/10oz chopped frozen spinach*
*450g/1lb minced/ground pork*
*1 onion, peeled and chopped*
*2 cloves garlic, crushed*
*60ml/4 tbsps chopped fresh mixed herbs*
*180ml/6 fl oz/⅔ cup double/heavy cream*
*1 small can ham cut in 1.25cm/½ inch thick strips*
*225g/8oz bacon*
*Salt and pepper*
*1 egg, beaten*

Cook the spinach in a large bowl or casserole for 5 minutes on HIGH,

**This page: Pâté aux Herbes. Facing page: Stuffed Mushrooms (top) and Chicken and Tongue Rolls (bottom).**

breaking it up as it cooks. Drain well to remove any excess water. Combine with the pork, onion, garlic, herbs, cream and salt and pepper. Add the egg and stir thoroughly together. Line a 450g/1lb glass loaf dish with the strips of bacon. Press ½ of the pork and spinach mixture into the dish on top of the bacon. Lay the ham strips on top. Repeat with remaining spinach and pork mixture. Cover the dish well and cook for 20 minutes on MEDIUM. Leave to stand until cool. Place a weight on top of the dish and leave in the refrigerator for 2 hours, or until firm. Cover tightly and freeze for up to 2 months. To defrost, heat gently on LOW or DEFROST for 10 minutes, rearranging the dish occasionally and not allowing the mixture to get too hot. Leave to stand for 10 minutes and then repeat the process until defrosted. Allow to cool and serve with salad and French bread.

*Microwave*

## FREEZER TO MICROWAVE

# MAIN MEALS

## Stuffed Peppers

**PREPARATION TIME:** 20 minutes

**MICROWAVE COOKING TIME:**
28-31 minutes

**SERVES:** 4-6 people

3 large peppers, red, yellow and green
   variety
340g/¾ lb minced/ground beef
1 onion, finely chopped
60g/2oz/½ cup rice, cooked
60g/2oz/½ cup raisins
30g/2 tbsps chopped walnuts
15ml/1 tbsp Worcestershire sauce
10ml/2 tsps brown sugar
10ml/2 tsps wine vinegar
Salt and pepper

**SAUCE**
450g/1lb canned tomatoes
1 bay leaf
10ml/2 tsps chili powder
1 clove garlic, crushed
15ml/1 tbsp tomato purée/paste
15ml/1 tbsp cornflour/cornstarch mixed
   with 30ml/2 tbsps water
Salt and pepper

Cut the peppers in half and remove
the cores and seeds. Place them in
1 layer in a shallow dish with 60ml/
4 tbsps water. Cover loosely and
cook for 4 minutes on HIGH. Leave
to stand, covered, while preparing
the filling. Cook the beef for 5-6
minutes on MEDIUM in a casserole
dish. Add the onion and increase the
setting to HIGH. Cook 4-6 minutes
further, breaking the meat up with a
fork frequently while cooking. Stir in
the remaining ingredients. Drain the
peppers and fill with the meat.
Combine all the sauce ingredients
except the cornflour/cornstarch in
water, in a glass measure. Cook for

12 minutes on HIGH, or until
boiling. Combine the cornflour/
cornstarch and water and stir into
the sauce. Cook a further 3 minutes,
stirring frequently after 1 minute.
Allow to cool slightly, remove the
bay leaf and purée the sauce. Strain if
desired. Pour over the peppers in a
serving dish and allow to cool. Cover

**This page: Chicken Paprika. Facing
page: Stuffed Peppers.**

well and freeze for up to 3 months.
Defrost 10-15 minutes on LOW or
DEFROST and allow to stand for
10 minutes. Cook 10 minutes on
HIGH to reheat and serve.

## Beef Ragôut

**PREPARATION TIME:** 20 minutes

**MICROWAVE COOKING TIME:**
29 minutes

**SERVES:** 4 people

30ml/2 tbsps oil
450g/1lb frying steak
15ml/1 tbsp flour
1 clove garlic, crushed
140ml/¼ pint/½ cup red wine
280ml/½ pint/1 cup beef stock
Bouquet garni (1 sprig thyme, 1 bay leaf,
    3 parsley stalks)
Salt and pepper
5ml/1 tsp tomato purée/paste (optional)
2 large carrots, peeled and cut into
    matchsticks
2 roots of salsify, peeled and cut into
    matchsticks
2 small leeks, thinly sliced and well
    washed
120g/4oz mushrooms, quartered

Heat a browning dish according to
the manufacturer's directions.
Meanwhile trim the meat and cut it
into 2.5cm/1 inch pieces. Pour the oil
into the browning dish and quickly
brown the meat on all sides. Pour the
meat juices and oil into a casserole
dish and mix in the flour. Add the
garlic and gradually stir in the wine
and the stock. Add the bouquet
garni, cover the dish and cook on
HIGH for 6 minutes, stirring every
2 minutes until thickened. Add the
meat and the bouquet garni to the
dish and re-cover. Cook on HIGH
for a further 15 minutes, or until the
meat is tender. Adjust the seasoning
and leave the casserole to stand,
covered. Meanwhile, place the carrot
and the salsify in a small bowl with
60ml/4 tbsps water. Cover and cook
on HIGH for 4 minutes. Add the
leeks and the mushrooms and re-
cover the dish. Cook a further
4 minutes on HIGH, or until the
vegetables are tender. Drain. Remove
the bouquet garni from the meat and
allow the meat to cool completely.
Allow the vegetables to cool
completely and freeze the meat and
the vegetables in separate containers
for up to 3 months. To defrost, heat
the meat for 6-8 minutes on LOW or
DEFROST, breaking up the chunks

of meat as they defrost. Allow to
stand 10-20 minutes before reheating.
Defrost the vegetables on LOW or
DEFROST for 4 minutes and leave
to stand before reheating. To reheat,
combine the vegetables and the meat
in a serving dish and cover well.
Cook on HIGH for 12-15 minutes
until heated through. Serve with rice,
pasta or potatoes.

## Spiced Pork Casserole

**PREPARATION TIME:** 15 minutes

**MICROWAVE COOKING TIME:**
16-21 minutes

**SERVES:** 4 people

30ml/2 tbsps oil
450g/1lb pork fillet, cut in 2.5cm/1 inch
    cubes
1 onion, finely sliced
1.25ml/¼ tsp ground turmeric
2.5ml/½ tsp ground coriander
1.25ml/¼ tsp ground allspice
30ml/2 tbsps flour
280ml/½ pint/1 cup chicken or vegetable
    stock
Juice and grated rind of 1 orange
Salt and pepper
8 dried apricots
30g/2 tbsps sultanas/golden raisins
30ml/2 tbsps currants

Heat a browning dish according to
the manufacturer's directions. When
hot, add half the oil and quickly
brown the pork on all sides. Place the
onion in a large bowl or casserole
with the remaining oil, cover loosely
and cook on HIGH for 3 minutes.
Stir in the spices and the flour and
then add the stock, orange juice and
rind and cover the bowl. Cook on
HIGH for a further 3 minutes. Stir
well and add the contents of the
browning dish, salt and pepper and
the dried fruit. Cook, uncovered, on
HIGH for 10-15 minutes, stirring
several times during cooking. Adjust
the seasoning and allow to cool
completely. Fill a serving dish or a
freezer container with the casserole
and seal well. Freeze for up to
2 months. To defrost, keep the
casserole covered and heat on LOW
or DEFROST for 4-6 minutes,

breaking-up large pieces of the
casserole as it defrosts. Allow to
stand, covered, for 10-20 minutes
before reheating. Reheat on HIGH
for 12-14 minutes and serve with rice.

## Chicken Paprika

**PREPARATION TIME:** 20 minutes

**MICROWAVE COOKING TIME:**
36-47 minutes plus standing time

**SERVES:** 4 people

1.25kg/3¼ lbs chicken, cut into 8 pieces
    and skinned
45ml/3 tbsps oil
1 medium onion, finely sliced
1 clove garlic, crushed
1 red pepper, seeded and thinly sliced
15ml/1 tbsp mild paprika
Pinch cayenne pepper (optional)
140ml/¼ pint/½ cup chicken stock
125g/8oz canned tomatoes, broken-up
Salt and pepper
15ml/1 tbsp cornflour/cornstarch mixed
    with 30ml/2 tbsps cold water

**GARNISH**
Natural yogurt or sour cream if desired

Place the oil and onion in a large
casserole dish and cook on HIGH for
3 minutes. Add the garlic, peppers,
paprika, cayenne pepper if using and
salt and pepper. Cover and cook on
HIGH for 2 minutes. Pour in the
stock and tomatoes and stir well.
Add the chicken and cook on
MEDIUM for 30-40 minutes. Blend
the cornflour/cornstarch and the
water and add to the chicken, stirring
well. Cook for 6-7 minutes on
MEDIUM or until the sauce
thickens. Allow to stand for
5 minutes. Allow to cool completely
and transfer to a serving dish or
freezer container. Cover well and
store for up to 2 months. To thaw
and reheat, cook, uncovered, on
LOW or DEFROST for 15 minutes,
stirring frequently. Leave to stand
10 minutes and reheat on HIGH for

**Facing page: Beef Ragôut (top) and
Spiced Pork Casserole (bottom).**

hot, pour in the oil and add the cubes of lamb, stirring to brown. Add the garlic and the spices and cook for 5 minutes on HIGH, stirring frequently. Pour the contents of the browning dish into a casserole, add the onions and sprinkle on the flour. Stir to mix thoroughly and pour on the stock. Add tomato purée/paste. Cover and cook on HIGH for 10 minutes. Stir in the peppers and the onions and cook for a further 10 minutes on HIGH. Allow to cool completely and put into a freezer container or a serving dish. Freeze for up to 3 months. Microwave on LOW or DEFROST for 5 minutes breaking-up the ingredients as they defrost. Allow the curry to stand for 5 minutes and then repeat the defrosting for another 5 minutes. Leave to stand 10 minutes. Repeat if necessary. When completely defrosted, stir in the coconut and heat for 8 minutes on HIGH. Add the yogurt and the tomatoes and cook for a further 2 minutes on HIGH, or until heated through. Serve with rice.

## Chicken Korma

**PREPARATION TIME:** 15 minutes

**MICROWAVE COOKING TIME:** 20 minutes

**SERVES:** 4 people

30g/2 tbsps butter or margarine
1 onion, chopped
2 apples, peeled, cored and chopped
15ml/1 tbsp curry paste
15ml/1 tbsp flour
280ml/½ pint/1 cup chicken or vegetable stock
5ml/1 tsp lime juice
5ml/1 tsp tomato purée/paste (optional)
450g/1lb chicken, skinned, boned and diced
Salt and pepper
60g/2oz/½ cup roasted cashews
140ml/¼ pint/½ cup natural yogurt

10-12 minutes. When thoroughly hot, spoon yogurt or sour cream over the top, if using, and serve with pasta.

## Lamb Masala

**PREPARATION TIME:** 15 minutes

**MICROWAVE COOKING TIME:** 30 minutes

**SERVES:** 4 people

15ml/1 tbsp oil
450g/1lb lamb fillet, cut into 2.5cm/ 1 inch pieces
2 cloves garlic, crushed
10ml/2 tbsps garam masala

5ml/1 tsp ground cumin
5ml/1 tsp ground coriander
2.5ml/½ tsp ground ginger
Pinch ground cloves
Pinch ground cinnamon
1 small red pepper, seeded and sliced
1 small green pepper, seeded and sliced
1 onion, sliced
25ml/1½ tbsps flour
140ml/¼ pint/½ cup stock
10ml/2 tsps tomato purée/paste
10ml/2 tsps desiccated coconut
30ml/2 tbsps natural yogurt
3 tomatoes, quartered and cored
Salt and pepper

Heat a browning dish according to the manufacturer's directions. When

**This page: Spicy Lamb Chops.
Facing page: Lamb Masala (top) and
Chicken Korma (bottom).**

Melt the butter for 30 seconds on HIGH in a bowl. Add the onion and apples and cook, uncovered, on HIGH for 4 minutes, stirring occasionally. Add the curry paste, flour, stock, lime juice and tomato purée/paste if using. Stir together well and cook on HIGH for 2 minutes. Stir in the diced chicken and cover the bowl. Cook on HIGH for 3 minutes and then stir well. Cook a further 3-5 minutes on HIGH until the apple has disintegrated and the chicken is cooked. Stir in the cashews and allow the curry to cool completely. Put into a freezer container or a serving dish, cover well and freeze for up to 2 months. Heat for 5 minutes on LOW or DEFROST, breaking-up the ingredients as they defrost. Leave the curry to stand for 5 minutes and then heat again on LOW or DEFROST for 5 minutes, or until completely defrosted. Leave to stand 10 minutes to complete defrosting. Reheat for 8 minutes on HIGH and stir in the yogurt. Cook a further 2 minutes on HIGH and serve with rice or poppadums. To prepare poppadums in the microwave oven, brush each side lightly with oil and cook one at a time on HIGH for about 30 seconds, or until crisp.

## Piquant Liver

**PREPARATION TIME:** 20 minutes

**MICROWAVE COOKING TIME:** 14-15 minutes

**SERVES:** 4 people

*30g/2 tbsps butter or margarine*
*2 onions, thinly sliced*
*30g/2 tbsps flour mixed with a good*
  *pinch of salt and pepper*
*450g/1lb lambs' or calves' liver, thinly*
  *sliced*
*140ml/¼ pint/½ cup beef stock*
*30ml/2 tbsps white wine vinegar*
*2.5ml/½ tsp marjoram*
*15ml/1 tbsp chopped parsley*

Put the butter or margarine and the onions into a bowl and cook on HIGH for 2-3 minutes, stirring occasionally. Skin the liver and remove any large ducts or tubes. Toss

in the seasoned flour and shake off the excess. Mix any remaining flour with the stock and vinegar. Layer the liver and onions in a shallow baking dish. Add the marjoram and parsley to the stock mixture and pour over the liver. Cover the dish with pierced cling film/plastic wrap and cook on HIGH for 10-12 minutes, stirring occasionally. Allow to cool completely before wrapping and freezing. Store up to 6 weeks. To defrost, microwave on LOW or DEFROST for 8-10 minutes and allow to stand for about 10 minutes. Reheat on HIGH for 10-12 minutes, stirring occasionally. Serve with saffron rice.

## Kidneys Turbigo

**PREPARATION TIME:** 15 minutes

**MICROWAVE COOKING TIME:** 20 minutes

**SERVES:** 4 people

*15ml/1 tbsp oil*
*225g/8oz small pork sausages, skins*
  *pricked all over*
*12 lambs' kidneys, halved and cored*
*225g/8oz button onions, peeled*
*120g/4oz small mushrooms, left whole*
*280ml/½ pint/1 cup beef stock*
*15ml/1 tbsp tomato purée/paste*
*30ml/2 tbsps sherry*
*1 bay leaf*
*1.25ml/¼ tsp thyme*
*30ml/2 tbsps cornflour/cornstarch*
  *dissolved in 60ml/4 tbsps cold water*
*15ml/1 tbsp chopped parsley*
*Salt and pepper*

Heat a browning dish according to the manufacturer's directions. Add the oil and cook for 30 seconds on HIGH. Add the sausages and cook on HIGH for about 5 minutes, turning over several times during cooking, until lightly browned. Remove the sausages from the browning dish to a casserole. Reheat the dish and brown the onions lightly. Add the onions to the sausages in the casserole along with the kidneys and the mushrooms. Pour over the stock and stir in the tomato purée/paste. Add the sherry, bay leaf, thyme and salt and pepper

and cover the dish. Cook on HIGH for about 12 minutes, stirring frequently. Add the cornflour/cornstarch and water mixture to the casserole and stir very well. Cook, uncovered, about 3 minutes or until the sauce thickens. Stir frequently after 1 minute. Remove the bay leaf and allow the casserole to cool completely. Freeze in the casserole dish or another serving dish. Cover well and keep in the freezer for up to 6 weeks. To defrost, warm on LOW or DEFROST for 10-12 minutes, with a 3 minute interval after each 5 minutes of defrosting. Reheat for 7-10 minutes on HIGH and garnish with chopped parsley.

## Spicy Lamb Chops

**PREPARATION TIME:** 20 minutes

**MICROWAVE COOKING TIME:** 17½-19½ minutes

**SERVES:** 4 people

*30ml/2 tbsps oil*
*5ml/1 tsp ground cumin*
*5ml/1 tsp ground coriander*
*5ml/1 tsp chili powder*
*15ml/1 tbsp red wine vinegar*
*60ml/4 tbsps orange juice*
*15ml/1 tbsp soft brown sugar*
*5ml/1 tsp tomato purée/paste*
*5ml/1 tsp Worcestershire sauce*
*280ml/½ pint/1 cup beef or chicken*
  *stock*
*4 lamb chump chops*
*1 onion, sliced*
*1 small red and 1 small green pepper,*
  *seeded and sliced*
*60g/2oz salted peanuts*
*Pepper*
*30ml/2 tbsps cornflour/cornstarch mixed*
  *with 60ml/4 tbsps water*

Heat the oil in a shallow dish for 30 seconds on HIGH. Stir in the spices and all the remaining marinade ingredients. Heat for 2 minutes on HIGH and set aside to cool. When cold, place in the lamb chops and turn them once or twice to coat

**Facing page: Kidneys Turbigo (top) and Piquant Liver (bottom).**

## Veal with Fennel and Tomato

**PREPARATION TIME:** 15 minutes

**MICROWAVE COOKING TIME:** 16-21 minutes

**SERVES:** 4 people

*30ml/2 tbsps oil*
*450g/1lb lean veal, cut into 2.5cm/ 1 inch cubes*
*1 medium onion, finely sliced*
*1.25ml/¼ tsp fennel seed, crushed*
*5ml/1 tsp chopped basil*
*1 bay leaf*
*1 clove garlic, crushed*
*360g/12oz canned plum tomatoes*
*10ml/2 tsps tomato purée/paste*
*140ml/¼ pint/½ cup red wine*
*30ml/2 tbsps cornflour/cornstarch*
*1 bulb fennel, trimmed and thinly sliced*

Heat a browning dish according to the manufacturer's instructions. When hot, add the oil to the dish and quickly brown the veal on all sides. Remove the veal, add the onions to the dish and stir to brown lightly. Transfer the veal and onions to a casserole dish and add the fennel seed, basil, bay leaf and garlic. Stir in the canned tomatoes and the tomato purée/paste. Cover the dish and cook on HIGH for 10-15 minutes, stirring halfway through cooking. Add salt and pepper and leave to stand while preparing the fennel. Put the fennel slices into a small bowl or casserole with 60ml/4 tbsps water. Cover and cook for 6 minutes on HIGH. Leave both the veal and the fennel to cool and pack them separately into freezer containers. Freeze for up to 2 months. To defrost, follow the instructions for Beef Ragôut. When defrosted, combine the fennel and the veal in a serving dish, cover, and cook on HIGH for 12-15 minutes, or until heated through. Serve with rice or pasta.

## Chicken Dijon

**PREPARATION TIME:** 15 minutes plus overnight soaking for lentils

---

evenly. Leave to marinate for about 1 hour in the refrigerator. Heat a browning dish according to the manufacturer's instructions. When hot, lift the chops from the marinade and drain them. Place them on the hot browning dish and press down firmly. Cook, uncovered, for 5 minutes on HIGH. Turn the chops over and lower the temperature to MEDIUM or ROAST and cook for 3-4 minutes. Set aside to cool. Meanwhile, combine the remaining marinade with the onions and the peppers. Cook, uncovered, for 5 minutes on HIGH and add the cornflour/cornstarch and water mixture. Stir well and cook 2-3 minutes or until thickened. Add the

**This page: Prawn/Shrimp and Chicken Pilaf. Facing page: Veal with Fennel and Tomato (top) and Chicken Dijon (bottom).**

peanuts and allow the sauce to cool. Arrange the lamb chops in a serving dish that will go into the freezer. Pour over the cooled sauce and cover well. Freeze for up to 2 months. To reheat, microwave on LOW or DEFROST for 5 minutes. Allow the dish to stand for 5 minutes and then repeat the defrosting for a further 5 minutes or until completely defrosted. To reheat, microwave on HIGH for 10-15 minutes or until all the ingredients are hot.

**MICROWAVE COOKING TIME:**
21-26 minutes

**SERVES:** 4 people

30ml/2 tbsps oil
675g/1½ lbs chicken pieces, skinned
12 button onions
15ml/1 tbsp flour
340ml/¾ pint/1½ cups chicken stock
30ml/2 tbsps Dijon mustard
5ml/1 tsp coarsely ground black pepper
120g/4oz red lentils
Salt
Bouquet garni
15ml/1 tbsp chopped parsley

Heat a browning dish according to the manufacturer's directions. Pour the oil into the browning dish when it is hot and add the chicken pieces, a few at a time. Turn them to brown quickly on all sides and remove them to a bowl. Reheat the browning dish and brown the button onions quickly and place them with the chicken. Add the flour to the browning dish and cook 1 minute on HIGH to brown slightly. Pour over some of the chicken stock to deglaze the browning dish and add to the chicken. Pour over the remaining stock and stir in the Dijon mustard and coarsely ground black pepper. Add the lentils, salt and bouquet garni. Cover loosely and cook on HIGH for 15-20 minutes, stirring occasionally. Allow to cool and remove the bouquet garni. Arrange in a serving dish and cover well. Freeze for up to 2 months. Defrost for 10-12 minutes on a LOW or DEFROST setting. Allow the chicken to stand for 3-5 minutes at 5 minute intervals during defrosting if the outside edges of the casserole begin cooking before the middle has defrosted. Reheat on HIGH for 10-12 minutes and sprinkle with the chopped parsley before serving. Serve with potatoes or pasta.

## Fisherman's Pie

**PREPARATION TIME:** 15 minutes

**MICROWAVE COOKING TIME:**
26-28 minutes

**SERVES:** 4 people

450g/1lb fish and shellfish (mixture of whitefish, smoked fish, prawns/shrimp and mussels)
675g/1½ lbs potatoes, peeled
30g/2 tbsps butter or margarine
60ml/4 tbsps hot milk
Salt and pepper

**SAUCE**
30g/2 tbsps butter or margarine
30g/2 tbsps flour
Milk
45ml/3 tbsps chopped parsley
Dash tabasco
Salt and pepper

**GLAZE**
1 egg, beaten with a pinch of salt

Skin the fish and remove any bones. Cut into chunks, place in a large bowl and cover with pierced cling film/plastic wrap. Cook on HIGH for 4 minutes. Add the mussels to the bowl and cook for a further 2 minutes on HIGH. Leave to stand, covered, while preparing the potatoes. Place the potatoes in a bowl with 60ml/4 tbsps water, cover and cook on HIGH for 10-12 minutes or until tender. Drain well and mash with butter and hot milk until smooth. Season with salt and pepper. Melt the butter for the sauce in a glass measure for 30 seconds on HIGH. Stir in the flour and measure the juices from the fish. Make up to 280ml/½ pint/1 cup with cold milk. Stir the milk and fish juices into the flour and butter and whisk well. Cook on HIGH for 6 minutes, whisking several times during cooking to prevent lumps from forming. Stir in the parsley and add salt and pepper and a dash of tabasco. Arrange the fish and mussels in a casserole dish and add the prawns/shrimp. Pour the sauce over the fish and smooth down. Spoon or pipe the mashed potato on top in a lattice pattern. Allow the pie to cool completely and then freeze until the potato is firm. Cover the pie well and freeze up to 2 months. Heat the pie for 10 minutes on LOW or DEFROST, leaving a 3 minute interval between each 5 minute defrosting period. Glaze the potato with the beaten egg and cook on HIGH for 12-15 minutes, or until

heated through. Brown under a preheated grill/broiler before serving.

## Cauliflower and Ham Mornay

**PREPARATION TIME:** 15 minutes

**MICROWAVE COOKING TIME:**
18-25 minutes

**SERVES:** 4 people

1 medium sized cauliflower, broken into large flowerets
120g/4oz ham, cut into cubes or strips

**MORNAY SAUCE**
30g/2 tbsps butter or margarine
30g/2 tbsps flour
280ml/½ pint/1 cup milk
Salt and pepper
Dash Worcestershire sauce
Dash tabasco
120g/4oz/1 cup Cheddar cheese, grated

Place the cauliflower flowerets in a bowl or casserole with 45ml/3 tbsps water. Cover and cook on HIGH for 10-15 minutes, stirring gently occasionally. Drain the cauliflower and mix with the ham. Arrange in a shallow serving dish. Melt the butter or margarine for the sauce in a glass measure for 1-2 minutes on HIGH. Stir in the flour and gradually beat in the milk. Cook on HIGH for 7-8 minutes, whisking occasionally to prevent lumps from forming. Season with salt and pepper, Worcestershire sauce and tabasco. Stir in half the cheese. Pour the sauce over the cauliflower and ham and sprinkle on the remaining cheese. To freeze, allow to cool completely and cover well. Freeze for up to 1 month. To defrost, heat on LOW or DEFROST for 15-20 minutes, taking the dish out of the oven and leaving it to stand for 2-3 minutes at 5 minute intervals if outside edges begin to cook before the middle is defrosted. To reheat, cook on HIGH for 5-7 minutes and brown under a hot grill/broiler if desired.

**Facing page: Fisherman's Pie (top) and Cauliflower and Ham Mornay (bottom).**

## Chicken Veracruz

**PREPARATION TIME:** 25 minutes

**MICROWAVE COOKING TIME:**
38 minutes

**SERVES:** 4 people

450g/1lb chicken, skinned and boned
30ml/2 tbsps oil
2 medium onions, diced
10ml/2 tsps chili powder
1 clove garlic, crushed
10ml/2 tsps dried oregano
10ml/2 tsps cumin seed, slightly crushed
5ml/1 tsp cayenne pepper
Salt
15ml/1 tbsp cornflour/cornstarch mixed
    with 30ml/2 tbsps water
280ml/½ pint/1 cup chicken stock
125g/8oz canned tomatoes
425g/15oz canned chickpeas, drained
    and rinsed
1 small red pepper, seeded and diced
1 small green pepper, seeded and diced
1 small yellow pepper, seeded and diced

Cut the chicken into small cubes.
Place the oil and the onions in a bowl
with the chili powder and cook on
HIGH for 3 minutes or until the
onion softens. Add the remaining
ingredients except the chickpeas and
peppers and stir well. Cover and
cook on HIGH for 10 minutes. Turn
down to LOW or DEFROST and
cook for 20 minutes or until the
chicken is tender. Add the chickpeas
and peppers and cook for a further
5 minutes on HIGH. Allow to cool
completely before transferring to a
serving dish or a freezer container.
Cover well and store for up to
2 months. To thaw and reheat, cook
on LOW or DEFROST for 10-12
minutes, stirring from time to time.
Leave to stand 10 minutes. Reheat on
HIGH 7-10 minutes. Serve with rice.

## Pork Normande

**PREPARATION TIME:** 20 minutes

**MICROWAVE COOKING TIME:**
48 minutes

**SERVES:** 4 people

30g/2 tbsps butter or margarine
2-3 pork fillets, thinly sliced
2 shallots, finely chopped

1 cooking apple, peeled, cored and
    chopped
140ml/¼ pint/½ cup dry cider
140ml/¼ pint/½ cup chicken or vegetable
    stock
5ml/1 tsp lemon juice
5ml/1 tsp crumbled sage
Salt and pepper
60g/2oz/½ cup sultanas/white raisins
15ml/1 tbsp cornflour/cornstarch mixed
    with 30ml/2 tbsps water
60ml/4 tbsps double/heavy cream

**GARNISH** (after defrosting)
2 apples, cored and thinly sliced
60g/2 tbsps brown sugar
30ml/2 tbsps chopped parsley

Pre-heat a browning dish according
to the manufacturer's directions.
When hot, melt the butter and add
the pork and shallots and stir to
brown. Return the browning dish to
the oven and cook on HIGH for 5
minutes, stirring frequently. Pour the
contents of the browning dish into a
casserole and add the apple, cider,
stock, lemon juice, sage and salt and
pepper. Cover the dish and cook on
MEDIUM for about 40 minutes. Stir
the cornflour/cornstarch and water
mixture into the sauce and cook for
2-3 minutes on HIGH, or until
thickened. Add the cream and the
sultanas/raisins and stir well. Allow
to cool completely and then put into
a serving dish or freezer container.
Reserve the garnish for later use.
Freeze for up to 2 months. To
defrost, warm on LOW or
DEFROST for 5 minutes, breaking-
up the ingredients as they thaw.
Allow the pork to stand for 5
minutes and then repeat the process
until completely defrosted. To reheat,
cook on HIGH for 10-15 minutes. To
garnish, heat a browning dish
according to the manufacturer's
directions and when hot place on the
sliced apples. Sprinkle over the
brown sugar and turn the apples
frequently to glaze. Cook for
approximately 2-3 minutes on
HIGH. Arrange the apples on top of
the pork and sprinkle with chopped
parsley to serve.

## Prawn/Shrimp and Chicken Pilaf

**PREPARATION TIME:** 15 minutes

**MICROWAVE COOKING TIME:**
30-40 minutes

**SERVES:** 4-6 people

60g/2oz butter or margarine
340g/12oz chicken, skinned, boned and
   cut into thin shreds
1 onion, sliced
1 red pepper, seeded and sliced
1 green pepper, seeded and sliced
90g/3oz mushrooms sliced
60g/2oz unblanched almonds, roughly
   chopped
2 sticks celery, sliced
1 clove garlic, crushed
5ml/1 tsp turmeric
5ml/1 tsp basil, chopped
30ml/2 tbsps parsley, chopped
Salt and pepper
140g/12oz/1½ cups cooked rice
225g/8oz frozen peeled prawns/shrimp
60g/2oz/½ cup grated Parmesan cheese

**Facing page: Chicken Veracruz.
This page: Tarragon Chicken (top)
and Pork Normande (bottom).**

Melt the butter for 30 seconds on
HIGH in a large casserole. Add the
chicken and cover the dish. Cook on
HIGH for 6-8 minutes, stirring
occasionally. Add all the remaining
ingredients except the prawns/
shrimp, cheese and rice. Cook
together well and cook for a further
5 minutes on HIGH, stirring
occasionally. Stir in the rice and allow
the mixture to cool completely. Pack
into a freezer container, separately
from the prawns/shrimp and reserve
the cheese to finish. Freeze for up to
2 months. To defrost, warm on LOW
or DEFROST for 5 minutes,
breaking the ingredients up as they
defrost. Leave to stand, covered, for
5 minutes and heat again on LOW or
DEFROST for a further 5 minutes or
until completely defrosted. Reheat
for 5 minutes on HIGH and stir in
the frozen prawns/shrimp. Reheat a
further 5 minutes on HIGH or until
all the ingredients are hot. Do not
over-cook the prawns. Sprinkle with
Parmesan cheese to serve.

## Tarragon Chicken

**PREPARATION TIME:** 10 minutes

**MICROWAVE COOKING TIME:**
19 minutes

**SERVES:** 4 people

60g/4 tbsps butter or margarine
1 clove garlic, crushed
2 shallots, finely chopped
60g/2oz small mushrooms, left whole
4 chicken breasts, skinned and boned
30ml/2 tbsps chopped fresh tarragon
Salt and pepper
280ml/½ pint/1 cup chicken stock
30ml/2 tbsps cornflour/cornstarch
140ml/¼ pint/½ cup double/heavy
   cream
Squeeze lemon juice

**GARNISH** (after defrosting)
Fresh tarragon sprigs

Heat the butter or margarine in a
large casserole dish for 1-2 minutes
on HIGH. Add the garlic, shallot and
mushrooms. Cover and cook on
HIGH for 2 minutes. Arrange the
chicken on top of the mushrooms
and sprinkle over the tarragon.
Reserve 60ml/4 tbsps chicken stock
to mix with the cornflour/cornstarch
and add the rest of the stock to the
chicken. Cover and cook on
MEDIUM or ROAST for
12 minutes. Stir occasionally during
cooking. Add the cornflour/
cornstarch and stock mixture to the
chicken and stir well. Cook for 2-3
minutes on HIGH, uncovered, or
until thickened. Stir in the double
cream and adjust the seasoning. Add
the lemon juice and allow the
chicken to cool completely. Put into
a freezer container or arrange in a
serving dish, cover well and freeze for
up to 2 months. To thaw, heat on
LOW or DEFROST for 5 minutes
and then leave to stand for 5
minutes. Repeat the process until
completely defrosted. To reheat, cook
on HIGH for 10-15 minutes, stirring
occasionally. Garnish with fresh
tarragon leaves before serving.

*Microwave*

## FREEZER TO MICROWAVE

# VEGETABLES AND SNACKS

## Ratatouille

**PREPARATION TIME:** 30 minutes

**MICROWAVE COOKING TIME:**
10-15 minutes

**SERVES:** 4-6 people

1 large aubergine/eggplant, sliced, scored
    and salted
450g/1lb courgettes/zucchini, thinly
    sliced
1 large onion, thinly sliced
1 green pepper, cored and thinly sliced
450g/1lb tomatoes, skinned and chopped
30ml/2 tbsps olive oil
1 clove garlic, crushed
5ml/1 tsp chopped thyme
10ml/2 tsps chopped basil
Salt and pepper

Rinse aubergine/eggplant and pat dry.
Mix all the ingredients together in a
large bowl. Cover with cling film/
plastic wrap and microwave on
HIGH for 10-15 minutes. Adjust the
seasoning and allow to cool
completely. Freeze in a serving dish
or deep container. To thaw, warm on
LOW or DEFROST for 10-12
minutes, breaking-up the ingredients
as they thaw. May be served hot or
cold. Reheat 5-7 minutes on HIGH.

## Stuffed Baked Potatoes

**PREPARATION TIME:** 30 minutes

**MICROWAVE COOKING TIME:**
19 minutes plus standing time

**SERVES:** 4-8 people

4 large potatoes, scrubbed but not peeled
30g/2 tbsps butter or margarine
2 shallots, finely chopped
4 strips bacon/smoked streaky bacon,
    diced

4 mushrooms, finely chopped
30ml/2 tbsps frozen peas
60g/2oz/½ cup grated Cheddar cheese
Paprika

Prick the potato skins well and then
arrange the potatoes on paper towels
on the oven turntable. Cook on
HIGH for 15 minutes, turning the
potatoes over and re-arranging after
half the cooking time. Wrap each
potato in foil and leave to stand

**This page: Stuffed Baked Potatoes.
Facing page: Aubergine/Eggplant
Parmesan (top) and Ratatouille
(bottom).**

5 minutes until soft. Melt the butter
in a small bowl and add the onion
and bacon and cook on HIGH for
2 minutes, until the onion has
softened and the bacon is brown.
Add the mushrooms and peas and
cook a further 2 minutes on HIGH.

Cut a large slice from the top of each potato and scoop out all the potato flesh, leaving a thin lining inside each shell. Mash the potato until smooth and add 45-60ml/3-4 tbsps milk. Add salt and pepper and mix in the butter and vegetable mixture. Fill each potato skin and allow to cool completely. Sprinkle with cheese and wrap each potato separately. Freeze for up to 1 month. To thaw, unwrap the potatoes and place them on paper towels on the oven turntable. Cover them loosely with cling film/plastic wrap and cook on HIGH for 9 minutes. Re-arrange once or twice during cooking. Remove the covering and sprinkle with paprika. Cook a further 1 minute on HIGH. Leave to stand 2-3 minutes before serving.

## Muffin Pizzas

**PREPARATION TIME:** 25 minutes

**MICROWAVE COOKING TIME:** 10-11 minutes

**SERVES:** 4-8 people

225g/8oz canned tomatoes, drained
1 clove garlic, crushed
1.25ml/¼ tsp oregano
1.25ml/¼ tsp basil
15ml/1 tbsp tomato purée/paste
Salt and pepper
4 muffins, split
4 slices salami, chopped
60g/2oz mushrooms, sliced
180g/6oz/1½ cups grated Mozzarella cheese
30g/2 tbsps Parmesan cheese

Place the tomatoes, garlic, herbs, tomato purée/paste and seasoning in a bowl. Cover loosely and cook on HIGH for 4-5 minutes until thick, stirring once or twice. Leave to cool. Spread some of the tomato mixture on each muffin half and sprinkle over the chopped salami and mushrooms. Top with Mozzarella cheese and Parmesan cheese. Wrap each muffin pizza separately and freeze for up to 1 month. To thaw, unwrap the pizza and place on a plate lined with paper towels. Cook on HIGH for 6 minutes, re-arranging the pizzas once or twice during cooking. Leave to stand for 2-3 minutes before serving.

## Sloppy Joes

**PREPARATION TIME:** 20 minutes

**MICROWAVE COOKING TIME:** 6-7 minutes

**SERVES:** 6-8 people

450g/1lb minced/ground beef and pork mixed
1 onion, finely chopped
300g/10oz can tomato soup
10ml/2 tsps Worcestershire sauce
1 green pepper, finely chopped
10ml/2 tsps Dijon mustard
5ml/1 tsp tomato ketchup
10ml/2 tsps cider vinegar
10ml/2 tsps brown sugar
Salt and pepper
4 baps or hamburger buns, frozen

Combine the minced/ground meats and the onion in a casserole dish and cook, uncovered, on HIGH for 6-7 minutes. Break-up the meat with a fork as it cooks. Strain off any fat or liquid. Stir in the soup, Worcestershire sauce, chopped pepper, mustard, ketchup, vinegar, sugar and salt and pepper. Allow to cool completely and seal in freezer container. Cover well and freeze for up to 2 months. Freeze the rolls separately. To thaw, uncover the container and cook on HIGH for 7-8 minutes stirring occasionally to break-up the ingredients. During the last minute or two of cooking, add the rolls, wrapped in paper towels. When the rolls have defrosted and are warm, split them and fill with the Sloppy Joe mixture.

## Aubergine/Eggplant Parmesan

**PREPARATION TIME:** 30 minutes

**MICROWAVE COOKING TIME:** 15-20 minutes

**SERVES:** 4 people

2 medium aubergines/eggplant, halved, scored and sprinkled with salt
30ml/2 tbsps oil
1 onion, finely chopped
1 clove garlic, crushed
1 green pepper, seeded and diced

430g/15oz canned tomatoes
5ml/1 tsp chopped basil
1.25ml/¼ tsp oregano
30ml/2 tbsps cornflour/cornstarch mixed with 60ml/4 tbsps red or white wine
Dash cayenne pepper
Salt and pepper
120g/4oz/1 cup grated Parmesan cheese
Paprika

Leave the aubergines/eggplant to stand for 30 minutes and then rinse and drain well. Scoop out the flesh, leaving a thin shell of aubergine/eggplant inside the skin. Chop the flesh and heat the oil in a casserole for 1 minute on HIGH. Add the onion and the aubergine/eggplant flesh and cook for 1 minute on HIGH. Pour in the tomatoes and add the garlic, green pepper and herbs. Cover and cook on HIGH for 10 minutes. Add salt and pepper and the cornflour/cornstarch and white wine mixture. Cook a further 3-5 minutes on HIGH, or until thickened. Spoon into the aubergine/eggplant shells and allow to cool completely. Sprinkle on the cheese and place the aubergines/eggplant into a serving dish. Cover well and freeze for up to 1 month. Defrost on LOW or DEFROST for 5 minutes. Sprinkle on paprika and cook on HIGH for 7 minutes, or until hot and the cheese has melted. May be browned under pre-heated grill/broiler if desired.

## Tricolour Vegetable Purées

**PREPARATION TIME:** 25 minutes

**MICROWAVE COOKING TIME:** 21-27 minutes

**SERVES:** 6-8 people

**LEEK PURÉE**
900g/2lbs leeks, trimmed and well washed
30g/2 tbsps butter
30ml/2 tbsps double/heavy cream
Salt and pepper
Pinch nutmeg

**Facing page: Sloppy Joes (top) and Muffin Pizzas (bottom).**

then mash by hand or purée in a food processor until smooth. Beat in the butter, cream, salt, pepper and ground coriander. Allow all the purées to cool completely and freeze each separately in freezer containers. Cover well and keep for up to 1 month. Defrost each purée separately on LOW or DEFROST for 2 minutes and leave to stand for 5 minutes. Repeat the process until the purées are defrosted. Spoon the purées into a serving dish and cook on HIGH for 6-8 minutes until hot.

## Pommes Dauphinoise

**PREPARATION TIME:** 25 minutes

**MICROWAVE COOKING TIME:** 15-16 minutes

**SERVES:** 4-6 people

15g/1 tbsp butter
450g/1lb potatoes, peeled and thinly
    sliced
Salt and pepper
2 cloves garlic, crushed
280ml/½ pint/1 cup double/heavy
    cream
15ml/1 tbsp cornflour/cornstarch mixed
    with 30ml/2 tbsps cold milk
Paprika

Grease a round, shallow baking dish with the butter. Layer the potatoes into the dish with salt, pepper and garlic in between each layer. Mix the cream with the cornflour/cornstarch and milk mixture. Cook on HIGH for 3-4 minutes, stirring after 1 minute. Cook until thickened and pour over the potatoes. Sprinkle the top with paprika and cook on HIGH for 12 minutes. Allow to stand for 5 minutes and then cool completely. Cover the dish well and freeze for up to 3 weeks. Thaw on LOW or DEFROST for 10 minutes. Reheat on HIGH for 8 minutes without stirring.

## Honey and Lemon Parsnips

**PREPARATION TIME:** 10 minutes

**MICROWAVE COOKING TIME:** 10 minutes

### CARROT PURÉE
450g/1lb carrots, peeled and thinly sliced
1 sprig fresh thyme
30g/2 tbsps butter
30ml/2 tbsps double/heavy cream
Pinch sugar
Salt and pepper

### TURNIP PURÉE
450g/1lb turnips, peeled and roughly
    chopped
30g/2 tbsps butter
30ml/2 tbsps double/heavy cream
Salt and pepper
Pinch ground coriander

To prepare the leek purée, slice the leeks thinly and place in a bowl with 45ml/3 tbsps water. Cook on HIGH for 7-10 minutes, or until very tender. Drain and purée in a food processor until smooth. Add the butter, cream, salt, pepper and grated nutmeg and allow to cool completely. For the carrot purée, place the carrots in a bowl with the sprig of thyme and 45ml/3 tbsps water. Cover loosely and cook on HIGH for 6-8 minutes until tender. Drain and remove the sprig of thyme. Purée in a food processor until almost smooth. Beat in the butter, cream, sugar and salt and pepper to taste. The mixture will not be completely smooth. For the turnip purée, place the turnips in a bowl with 45ml/3 tbsps water. Cover and cook on HIGH for 8-9 minutes, or until very tender. Drain well and

**SERVES:** 4 people

450g/1lb young parsnips, peeled, trimmed
  and sliced
Rind and juice of 1 small lemon
45ml/3 tbsps honey
Pinch salt and pepper

Remove the cores from the parsnips
if they are tough. Combine the
parsnips with the remaining
ingredients in a large casserole and
cover with cling film/plastic wrap
pierced to release steam. Cook on
HIGH for 10 minutes and then allow
to stand for 2 minutes, covered.
Allow to cool completely and freeze
in a micro-proof serving dish. Cover
well and keep for up to 1 month.

**Facing page: Tricolour Vegetable
Purées (top) and Honey and Lemon
Parsnips (bottom). This page:
Pommes Dauphinoise (top) and
Pommes Duchesse (bottom).**

Thaw on LOW or DEFROST for
5 minutes and then leave to stand
until completely thawed at room
temperature. Reheat on HIGH for
5-8 minutes until very hot and glazed.

## Pommes Duchesse

**PREPARATION TIME:** 30 minutes

**MICROWAVE COOKING TIME:**
12-14 minutes

**SERVES:** 6-8 people

450g/1lb potatoes, scrubbed but not
  peeled
30ml/2 tbsps water
45-60ml/3-4 tbsps milk
1 large egg, beaten
Salt and pepper

Prick the skins of the potatoes with a
fork and place them with the water in
a casserole dish. Cover and cook on
HIGH for 10-12 minutes until tender.
Drain the potatoes, cut in half and
scoop out the flesh. Mash the
potatoes well with a potato masher
or with an electric whisk. Heat the
milk for 1 minute and add to the
potatoes with butter and seasoning.
Beat together well and leave to cool
completely. Mix in half the beaten
egg and fill a piping bag with the
potato mixture. Using a large rosette
nozzle/tube, pipe out swirls of potato
on a micro-proof baking sheet. Make
sure that the swirls of potato do not
have a hole in the centre. Cook on
HIGH for 1 minute. Brush with
beaten egg and cook a further
1 minute on HIGH, or until glaze has
set. Cool completely and freeze 2-3
hours, unwrapped. When solid, wrap
well and freeze for up to one month.
Reheat on HIGH for 3 minutes or
until piping hot. Brown quickly
under a pre-heated grill/broiler if
desired.

## Curried Vegetables

**PREPARATION TIME:** 30 minutes

**MICROWAVE COOKING TIME:**
13-16 minutes

**SERVES:** 6-8 people

15ml/1 tbsp oil
1 onion, finely chopped
1 green chili pepper, seeded and finely
  chopped
1 small piece fresh ginger, peeled and
  grated
2 cloves garlic, crushed
2.5ml/½ tsp ground coriander
2.5ml/½ tsp ground cumin
5ml/1 tsp ground turmeric
2 potatoes, peeled and diced
1 aubergine/eggplant, cut into small cubes
1 small cauliflower, cut into flowerets
390g/14oz canned tomatoes, drained

*140ml/¼ pint/½ cup vegetable or chicken stock*
*225g/8oz okra, trimmed and washed*
*120g/4oz/1 cup roasted, unsalted cashews*
*60g/4 tbsps desiccated coconut*
*60ml/4 tbsps natural yogurt*

Heat the oil in a large bowl or casserole dish for 1 minute on HIGH. Add the onion, chili pepper, ginger and garlic. Cook on HIGH for 1 minute further. Add the spices and cook an additional 1 minute on HIGH. Add the potatoes, aubergine/eggplant and tomatoes. Cover loosely and cook on HIGH for 8-10 minutes or until the potatoes and aubergine/eggplant are almost tender. Add the cauliflower, okra and stock. Cover loosely and cook on HIGH for 3-4 minutes, or until the vegetables are almost tender. Add the cashews and the desiccated coconut. Add salt and pepper to taste and allow the vegetables to cool

**This page: Curried Vegetables. Facing page: Almond Savarin.**

completely. Freeze in a container or a serving dish, well covered. Thaw on LOW or DEFROST for 10 minutes, stirring occasionally. Leave to stand 10 minutes, then reheat on HIGH for 6-10 minutes. Serve hot, topped with natural yogurt.

## FREEZER TO MICROWAVE

# BAKING AND DESSERTS

## Almond Savarin

**PREPARATION TIME:**
45 minutes-1 hour

**MICROWAVE COOKING TIME:**
18-21 minutes

**SERVES:** 6-8 people

60g/2oz/½ cup flaked/sliced almonds
225g/8oz strong/bread flour
5ml/1 tsp salt
120ml/4 fl oz/½ cup milk
10g/2 tsps fresh yeast, crumbled
10ml/2 tsps sugar
3 eggs, slightly beaten
90g/3oz/⅓ cup butter

**SYRUP**
140ml/¼ pint/½ cup water
90ml/6 tbsps amaretto
60ml/4 tbsps water
150g/5oz/⅔ cup sugar

**GARNISH**
Fresh fruit
Whipped cream

Place the almonds in a baking dish or a glass bowl and cook on HIGH for 6-8 minutes, shaking the bowl or dish occasionally. Once the almonds begin to brown, watch them carefully. Sift the flour and salt into a large, glass bowl and cook on HIGH for 20-30 seconds to warm the flour. Pour the milk into a glass measure and heat for 30 seconds on HIGH, or until lukewarm. Stir in the yeast and sugar until well mixed. Gradually beat in the eggs. Make a well in the centre of the flour and pour the yeast and egg mixture into the middle. Stir with a wooden spoon to gradually bring in the flour from the sides of the bowl and mix to a smooth batter. The batter will be slightly gluey and elastic. Cover the bowl with cling film/plastic wrap and warm for 10-15 seconds on HIGH to start the yeast working. Leave the bowl in a warm place until the batter doubles in bulk, about 45 minutes. Melt the butter on HIGH for 1 minute and allow to cool slightly. Beat into the risen batter with a wooden spoon until it is completely mixed in. Stir in the almonds. Once the mixture is smooth and elastic, pour into a well buttered microwave-proof ring mould, cover with cling film/plastic wrap and warm again for 10-15 seconds on HIGH. Leave to double in bulk, as before. Cook, uncovered, on HIGH for about 5-6 minutes until just firm to the touch. The top will still look moist. Allow to cool briefly in the dish and then turn out onto a wire rack to finish cooking

completely. Meanwhile combine the water and the amaretto with the sugar and stir well. Bring the mixture to the boil on HIGH. This takes about 5 minutes. Continue cooking for a further 2 minutes on HIGH. Allow the syrup to cool. Return the savarin to the cleaned ring mould and pierce all over with a skewer. Pour the syrup over the savarin and leave it to soak in. Turn the savarin out onto a plate or a very large freezer container and cool completely. Cover well and freeze for up to 2 months. To defrost, heat on HIGH for 1 minute and then leave to finish defrosting at room temperature. Fill the centre of the savarin with fresh fruit and cream to serve.

This page: Parfait au Cassis (top) and Frozen Wine Cream (bottom). Facing page: Burgundy Granita (right) and St. Clement's Sorbet (left).

## Burgundy Granita

**PREPARATION TIME:** 15 minutes

**MICROWAVE COOKING TIME:** 4 minutes

**SERVES:** 4-6 people

*90g/3oz/⅓ cup sugar, plus 30g/2 tbsps*
*Juice of ½ a lime and ½ an orange*
*15ml/1 tbsp water*
*½ bottle burgundy*

**GARNISH**
*Orange zest or blackberries or small bunches of red or blackcurrants*

Put the sugar, lime and orange juice and water into a deep bowl. Microwave on HIGH for 2 minutes, stir to help dissolve the sugar and microwave a further 2 minutes on HIGH. Cool and add the burgundy. Pour into a shallow freezer container and freeze until slushy. Spoon into a food processor or whisk with an electric mixer to break up ice crystals and then return to the freezer container, cover and freeze until solid. To serve, soften quickly in the microwave for 15-20 seconds on HIGH, keeping the container covered. Stir the mixture until crumbly and spoon into serving dishes. Decorate with orange zest or blackberries or the small bunches of red or blackcurrants.

## St. Clement's Sorbet

**PREPARATION TIME:** 20 minutes plus freezing

**MICROWAVE COOKING TIME:** 6 minutes

**SERVES:** 4-6 people

*250g/10oz/1¼ cups sugar*
*225ml/8 fl oz/1 cup water*
*4-5 lemons, depending upon size*
*4-6 oranges, depending upon size*
*60ml/4 tbsps orange liqueur*

**GARNISHES** *(to serve)*
*Citrus peel or mint leaves or desiccated coconut*

Combine the sugar and water in a large bowl. Cook, uncovered, on HIGH for about 5 minutes, or until boiling. Stir well and heat a further 1 minute on HIGH, or until the sugar dissolves. Allow to cool. Grate the rind of 1 lemon and 1 orange and add to the syrup. Squeeze the juice from the remaining lemons and oranges and strain into the syrup. Reserve strips of peel if desired for garnishing. Stir the liqueur into the syrup and chill. Freeze in ice cube trays until solid. To serve, place cubes in a food processor, 6-8 at a time, and process

quickly until smooth. Serve immediately. Prepare citrus peel garnish, scrape all the pith off the strips and then cut them into very fine shreds. Place them in a bowl with 30ml/2 tbsps water and cook on HIGH for 2 minutes to soften. Drain and dry. Sprinkle on top of the sorbet to serve. Alternatively, garnish with mint leaves or desiccated coconut. Keeps in the freezer, well sealed, for up to 3 months.

## Crêpes Suzette

**PREPARATION TIME:** 25 minutes

**MICROWAVE COOKING TIME:** 24 minutes

**SERVES:** 4-6 people

**PANCAKES**
120g/4oz/1 cup plain/all-purpose flour
Pinch salt
1 egg
280ml/½ pint milk
15ml/1 tbsp oil

**SAUCE**
90g/3oz/⅓ cup butter
60g/4 tbsps sugar
Grated rind and juice of 1 orange
Grated rind and juice of ½ lemon
60ml/4 tbsps brandy or orange liqueur

**GARNISH**
Thin orange slices

Sift the flour and salt into a bowl. Make a well in the centre and add the egg and half of the milk. Beat well, drawing in the flour from the sides of the bowl gradually. Gradually beat in the remaining milk and the oil. Allow the batter to stand for 30 minutes before using. Fry the pancakes in a small crêpe pan lightly greased with oil. Makes about 12-15 pancakes. Fold the pancakes into triangle shapes and arrange in a shallow dish. To make the sauce, put the butter into a glass measure and cook on DEFROST for 5 minutes, or until melted. Stir in the sugar to dissolve. Add the orange juice and rind, lemon juice and rind and the brandy or orange liqueur. Microwave on HIGH for 2 minutes and stir well. Pour over the pancakes and allow to cool completely. Cover

well with cling film/plastic wrap and freeze for up to 2 weeks. To thaw, cook on HIGH for 5 minutes. Leave to stand for 5 minutes and if necessary reheat a further 2-3 minutes on HIGH before serving. Garnish with thin orange slices. NOTE: pancakes may also be frozen separately, packed between pieces of greaseproof/wax paper or cling film/plastic wrap. Wrap well and freeze for up to 2 months. Thaw in the microwave oven for 2 minutes on LOW or DEFROST and then leave to stand at room temperature to finish defrosting.

## Parfait au Cassis

**PREPARATION TIME:** 25 minutes

**MICROWAVE COOKING TIME:** 12 minutes

**SERVES:** 6 people

340g/¾ lb/1½ cups blackcurrants, fresh or canned
30ml/2 tbsps Creme de Cassis
3 egg yolks
120g/4oz/1 cup soft brown sugar
280ml/½ pint/1 cup single/light cream
280ml/½ pint/1 cup double/heavy cream

**GARNISH**
Whole blackcurrants
Mint leaves

Purée the blackcurrants and sieve to remove the seeds. Add the cassis and freeze until slushy. Whisk the yolks and sugar until thick and mousse-like. Heat the single/light cream on HIGH for 2 minutes in an uncovered bowl. Add the cream gradually to the eggs and sugar, stirring constantly. Place the bowl in a dish of hot water. Water should be at the same level as the mixture. Loosely cover the bowl and heat on LOW for 10 minutes, stirring frequently. Cool quickly over ice, stirring occasionally. Whip the double/heavy cream and fold in. Freeze in a shallow container 2-3 hours, until almost solid. Quickly process or beat the cream mixture and pour it into a bowl. Process the blackcurrants and fold into the cream mixture for a marbled effect. Do not

over-fold. Freeze in glass micro-proof serving dishes. Soften in the refrigerator for 30 minutes before serving or warm on HIGH for 20 seconds. Garnish with blackcurrants and/or mint leaves. Serve with biscuits/cookies.

## Frozen Wine Cream

**PREPARATION TIME:** 20 minutes plus freezing

**MICROWAVE COOKING TIME:** 15 minutes

**SERVES:** 4-6 people

575g/1½ lbs white seedless grapes
430ml/¾ pint/1½ cups sweet white wine
180g/6oz/¾ cup sugar
430ml/¾ pint/1½ cups double/heavy cream, lightly whipped

Remove the grapes from the stems and place in a deep bowl with the wine. Cover loosely and cook on MEDIUM for 7 minutes, or until the grapes are soft. Remove from the oven and allow to cool completely. Purée in a food processor or blender and then sieve to remove the skins. Add food colouring if desired. Allow to cool completely and then mix with the cream. Place in a bowl or decorative mould and cover well. Freeze for up to 2 months. To defrost, allow to thaw at room temperature if the bowl or mould is metal. If the container is microwave-proof, warm on LOW or DEFROST for 2-3 minutes. Turn out and garnish with a small bunch of green grapes and mint leaves.

## Crêpes au Chocolat

**PREPARATION TIME:** 25 minutes

**MICROWAVE COOKING TIME:** 5 minutes

**SERVES:** 4-6 people

**PANCAKES**
Follow recipe for Crêpes Suzette

**Facing page: Crêpes au Chocolat (top) and Crêpes Suzette (bottom).**

Cover the dish loosely and cook on HIGH for 10 minutes. Stir the plums and set them aside to cool completely. Put the butter or margarine into a large mixing bowl. Cook on MEDIUM to MEDIUM HIGH for about 2 minutes, or until melted. Stir in the crushed biscuits and the almonds. Cook on HIGH for 2 minutes. Stir well after 1 minute. Carefully spoon the biscuit crumble over the plums. Allow the topping and plums to cool completely and then cover well. To thaw, microwave on DEFROST or LOW for 10 minutes, stand for 5 minutes and then microwave on HIGH for 5 minutes. Brown quickly under a grill/broiler if desired.

## Pineapple Upside-Down Cake

**PREPARATION TIME:** 20 minutes

**MICROWAVE COOKING TIME:**
8 minutes plus 5 minutes standing time

**SERVES:** 6 people

30g/2 tbsps butter
200g/7oz/¾ cup soft, light brown sugar
90g/3oz/¾ cup walnut halves
6-8 cocktail/maraschino cherries or glacé/candied cherries
225g/8oz canned sliced pineapple, well drained or fresh pineapple, peeled and sliced
120g/4oz/½ cup butter or margarine
2 eggs, beaten
120g/4oz/1 cup self-raising flour/ all-purpose flour with 1 tsp baking powder
60g/2oz/½ cup finely crushed digestive biscuits/graham crackers

Place the 30g/2 tbsps butter in a small glass bowl and melt for 30 seconds on HIGH. Stir in the sugar and heat a further 40-50 seconds on HIGH, or until the sugar has partially dissolved. Spread over the base of a

### FILLING
225g/8oz plain/semi-sweet chocolate, finely grated

### GARNISH
Icing/powdered sugar
Fresh or frozen raspberries

Prepare the pancakes as for the Crêpes Suzette recipe. Allow the pancakes to cool completely and fill each with the grated chocolate. Fold into triangles or roll-up into cigar shapes. Cover well and freeze for up to 1 month. To reheat, place on a serving dish and cover loosely. Cook on HIGH for 4-5 minutes until the pancakes are hot and the chocolate is melted. Allow to cool slightly, garnish with raspberries and sprinkle over sifted icing/powdered sugar.

## Plum and Ginger Crisp

**PREPARATION TIME:** 15 minutes

**MICROWAVE COOKING TIME:**
12 minutes

**SERVES:** 4-6 people

450g/1lb plums
90-120g/3-4oz demerara/raw sugar

### TOPPING
75g/5 tbsps butter or margarine
225g/8oz plain ginger biscuits/snaps, crushed
60g/2oz/½ cup flaked/sliced almonds

Wash, halve and stone the plums. Put into a micro-proof baking dish and toss with the sugar. If the plums are very sweet, do not add all the sugar.

**This page: Rum-Raisin Bread Pudding (top) and Plum and Ginger Crisp (bottom). Facing page: Pineapple Upside-Down Cake.**

20cm/8 inch round cake dish. Place 4-5 whole walnut halves in a circle in the middle of the dish. Cut cherries in half and place rounded side down in a circle around the walnuts. Cut pineapple rings in half and place half circles around the walnuts and cherries in a pinwheel design. Beat butter or margarine and remaining sugar until light and fluffy. Beat in the eggs gradually. Chop any remaining cherries, walnuts and pineapple and stir into the cake mixture. Sift in flour with the baking powder and stir in biscuit/cracker crumbs. Spoon carefully over the topping and smooth the top. Cook on HIGH for 6-7 minutes. When the cake is done it will pull away from the sides of the dish and a wooden pick/cocktail stick inserted into the centre will come out clean.

Cool completely, wrap and freeze in the baking dish for up to 3 months. To thaw, unwrap and re-heat in the baking dish on HIGH for 5 minutes. Leave to stand for 3 minutes before turning out onto a serving dish. Serve warm with cream, ice cream or lightly sweetened natural yogurt.

## Rum-Raisin Bread Pudding

**PREPARATION TIME:** 15 minutes plus soaking time

**MICROWAVE COOKING TIME:** 14 minutes

**SERVES:** 4 people

*570ml/1 pint/2 cups milk*
*225g/8oz wholemeal/whole-wheat bread*
*60ml/4 tbsps dark rum*
*120g/4oz/1 cup raisins*
*120g/4oz/½ cup demerara/raw sugar*
*15ml/1 tbsp golden syrup or honey*
*2 eggs, slightly beaten*
*60g/2oz butter or margarine*
*10ml/2 tsps mixed spice*

Pour the milk into a small bowl and heat for 1 minute on HIGH. Tear the bread into small pieces, put into the bowl with the milk and leave to stand for 2-3 hours to soak. Combine the rum and the raisins in a small bowl and heat for 1 minute on HIGH. Leave to stand while the bread soaks. Reserve half the sugar and combine the remaining half with the honey or golden syrup, eggs and 5ml/1 tsp mixed spice. Add to the bread mixture and stir well. Add the raisins and rum. Melt the butter or margarine on HIGH for 10-20 seconds and pour over the bread. Mix the butter or margarine in and pour into a lightly greased micro-proof baking dish. Cook on HIGH for 12-14 minutes, or until firm. Remove from the oven and sprinkle with the remaining sugar and mixed spice. To freeze, allow to cool completely and wrap well. Keep for up to 3 months. To thaw, heat on DEFROST or LOW for 3 minutes. Reheat on HIGH for 2 minutes.

## Fruit and Almond Cake

**PREPARATION TIME:** 20 minutes

**MICROWAVE COOKING TIME:** 13-16 minutes

**MAKES:** 1 cake

*180g/6oz/⅔ cup margarine*
*180g/6oz/¾ cup dark brown sugar*
*3 eggs, beaten*
*180g/6oz/1½ cups plain/all-purpose flour*
*10ml/2 tsps baking powder*
*2-3 drops almond essence/extract*
*30g/2 tbsps ground almonds*
*60g/2oz/½ cup seedless raisins*
*60g/2oz/½ cup dried apricots, roughly chopped*
*60g/2oz/½ cup glacé cherries, rinsed and roughly chopped*

Cream the margarine and sugar until light and fluffy. Add the beaten eggs, one at a time, beating well between each addition. Beat in the almond essence/extract and ground almonds and fold in the flour. Add the raisins, apricots and cherries. If the mixture is very thick, add enough milk to bring to dropping consistency. Lightly grease a large ring mould and sprinkle with sugar. Spoon the cake mixture into the prepared mould and smooth the top. Cook on MEDIUM HIGH for 12-14 minutes, increase the setting to HIGH and cook a further 1-2 minutes, or until just set. Allow to stand for 15 minutes and turn out onto a wire rack. Allow to cool completely and wrap well. Freeze for up to 3 months. To defrost, unwrap and cover with a paper towel. Warm on LOW or DEFROST for 5 minutes and then leave to stand to defrost at room temperature. When completely defrosted, sprinkle the top with a little sifted icing/powdered sugar.

## Banana-Date Walnut Loaf

**PREPARATION TIME:** 15 minutes

**MICROWAVE COOKING TIME:** 6 minutes

**MAKES:** 1 loaf

*2 eggs*
*60ml/4 tbsps milk*
*15ml/1 tbsp treacle/molasses*
*120g/4oz margarine*
*180g/6oz/1½ cups plain/all-purpose flour*
*10ml/2 tsps baking powder*
*90g/3oz/⅓ cup soft brown sugar*
*90g/3oz/⅓ cup chopped dates*
*1 small banana, sliced*
*60g/2oz/½ cup chopped walnuts*

Put the eggs, milk, treacle, margarine, flour and brown sugar into a large mixing bowl. Beat until well mixed. Add baking powder and fold in the dates, banana and walnuts. Spoon into a lightly greased 1.75 litre/3 pint/6 cup microwave bread dish. Cook on HIGH for about 6 minutes, giving the dish a half turn halfway through cooking time. Allow the bread to stand in the dish for 10 minutes before turning out. Allow to cool completely and wrap well. Freeze for up to 3 months. To defrost, unwrap and cover the loaf with paper towels. Thaw on LOW or DEFROST for 5 minutes and then leave to stand to continue defrosting at room temperature.

**Facing page: Fruit and Almond Cake (top) and Banana-Date Walnut Loaf (bottom).**

## Rhubarb Apricot Compôte

**PREPARATION TIME:** 10 minutes

**MICROWAVE COOKING TIME:**
6 minutes

**SERVES:** 4 people

*450g/1lb fresh young rhubarb, cut into
    2.5cm/1 inch pieces
Finely grated rind and juice of 1 orange
15ml/1 tbsp apricot jam
1 small can apricot halves*

Place the rhubarb, orange rind and
juice and the jam into a 850ml/
1½ pint/3 cup mixing bowl. Cover
loosely and cook on HIGH for
6 minutes. Stir well and set aside to
cool. Drain the apricots and chop
them roughly, reserving a few whole
for garnish, if desired. Add to the
rhubarb and chill. Put into a serving
dish or freezer container and cover
well. Freeze for up to 3 weeks. To
thaw, warm on LOW or DEFROST
for 12 minutes, breaking-up the fruit
gently as it defrosts. Leave to stand
for 10 minutes and then reheat for
1 minute on HIGH if desired.
Compôte may also be served cold
with yogurt, ice cream or whipped
cream.

## Apricot Pudding

**PREPARATION TIME:** 10 minutes

**MICROWAVE COOKING TIME:**
6-10 minutes

**SERVES:** 4-6 people

**BATTER**
*410g/14½ oz canned apricot halves
60g/4 tbsps butter or margarine
60g/4 tbsps sugar
1 egg, slightly beaten
120g/4oz/1 cup self-raising flour/
    all-purpose flour with 1 tsp baking
    powder
45-60ml/3-4 tbsps milk
Few drops almond essence/extract*

**SAUCE**
*Reserved apricots and juice
Juice of ½ lemon
15ml/1 tbsp cornflour/cornstarch*

Drain half the apricot halves well and

reserve the juice and the remaining
apricots. Chop the drained apricots
and set them aside. Beat the
margarine or butter to soften and
gradually beat in the sugar until light
and fluffy. Gradually add the egg,
beating well between each addition.
Sift in the flour with the baking
powder, if using, and fold together.
Stir in the chopped apricots and as
much milk as necessary to bring the
batter to dropping consistency. Add
the almond essence/extract. Grease a
570ml/1 pint/2 cup pudding basin or
micro-proof mixing bowl with
margarine and spoon in the pudding
batter, smoothing the top. Cook,
uncovered, for 3-5 minutes or until
the top is almost set but still moist.

**This page: Chocolate Cherry
Pudding (top) and Apricot Pudding
(bottom). Facing page: Poires Belle
Helene (top) and Rhubarb Apricot
Compôte (bottom).**

Leave the pudding to stand for
5 minutes. Allow to cool completely
and wrap well. Purée the apricots and
juice in a food processor or blender.
Add the lemon juice and cornflour/
cornstarch and mix well. Pour into a
glass measure and cook on HIGH for
3-5 minutes, or until thickened.
Cover the top of the sauce with a
circle of greaseproof/wax paper and
leave to cool completely. Pour the
sauce into a serving dish, jug or
freezer container and cover well.

Freeze the pudding and sauce separately for up to 3 months. To thaw the pudding, heat on LOW or DEFROST 1½-2 minutes and leave to stand for 10 minutes. Reheat on HIGH for 2 minutes. Heat the sauce on LOW or DEFROST for 2 minutes and leave to stand for 2 minutes. Reheat on HIGH for 1 minute. Turn out the pudding into a serving dish and pour over the sauce. Serve with whipped cream if desired.

## Jamaican Mousse Cake

**PREPARATION TIME:** 25 minutes

**MICROWAVE COOKING TIME:** 4 minutes

**SERVES:** 6-8 people

180g/6oz plain/semi-sweet chocolate
45ml/3 tbsps dark rum
140ml/¼ pint/½ cup double/heavy cream
15ml/1 tbsp strong black coffee
15g/1 tbsp demerara/raw sugar
2 large bananas, peeled and mashed until smooth
3 eggs, separated

**TO DECORATE**
140ml/¼ pint/½ cup cream, whipped
Chocolate curls

Break-up the chocolate, place in a bowl and cook on HIGH for 3 minutes, or until melted. Stir in the rum and cream and beat until smooth. Dissolve the sugar in the coffee for 1 minute on HIGH. Add to the chocolate mixture and beat in the bananas. Add the egg yolks, one at a time, beating well between each addition. Whisk the egg whites until stiff and then gently fold into the chocolate and banana mixture. Spoon into a loose-based or springform mould. Chill for 2 hours, cover and freeze for up to 1 month. Thaw at room temperature until mixture loosens from the sides. Unmould the mousse but leave on the base. If the base is metal, carefully slide the mousse off onto a serving plate. Use cream to decorate the top and add chocolate curls just before serving. Serve partially frozen.

## Chocolate Cherry Pudding

**PREPARATION TIME:** 10 minutes

**MICROWAVE COOKING TIME:** 8½ minutes

**SERVES:** 4-6 people

90g/3oz/⅓ cup softened butter or margarine
90g/3oz/⅓ cup soft brown sugar
90g/3oz/¾ cup self-raising flour/ all-purpose flour with 1 tsp baking powder
30g/2 tbsps cocoa
2 eggs
30ml/2 tbsps milk

**SAUCE**
420g/15oz morello cherries, drained and pitted
30ml/2 tbsps cornflour/cornstarch
30ml/2 tbsps kirsch (optional)
Few drops almond essence/extract

Beat the butter until softened and gradually beat in the sugar until light and fluffy. Lightly beat the eggs and add them gradually to the butter and sugar mixture. Sift the flour with the baking powder, if using, and the cocoa powder and fold in carefully. Add enough milk to bring the mixture to dropping consistency. Spoon into a lightly greased 850ml/ 1½ pint/3 cup micro-proof pudding basin. Cook on HIGH for 3½-4 minutes, until well risen and springy to the touch. Set aside to cool completely. Combine the cornflour/ cornstarch with the drained syrup from the cherries in a glass measure. Cook on HIGH for 3 minutes, stirring after 1 minute. When thickened, add the kirsch, if using, and almond essence/extract. Allow the sauce to cool completely and stir in cherries. Freeze the pudding and the sauce separately for up to 1 month. To thaw the pudding, heat on LOW or DEFROST for 1½-2 minutes and leave to stand for 10 minutes. Reheat on HIGH for 2 minutes. Heat the sauce on LOW or DEFROST for 2 minutes and leave to stand for 2 minutes. Reheat on HIGH for 1 minute. Turn the pudding out into a serving dish and pour over the sauce. Serve with whipped cream if desired.

## Poires Belle Helene

**PREPARATION TIME:** 20 minutes

**MICROWAVE COOKING TIME:** 7 minutes

**SERVES:** 4 people

280ml/½ pint/1 cup water
Juice of 1 small lemon
30g/2 tbsps sugar
4 ripe dessert pears, approximately the same size
120g/4oz plain/semi-sweet chocolate
45ml/3 tbsps double/heavy cream

**GARNISH**
Angelica or mint leaves
Whipped cream

Mix together the water, lemon juice and sugar in a bowl that will accommodate the 4 pears snugly. Peel the pears, leaving on the stems but removing the eyes in the bottom. Place pears stem side up in the bowl and cover with cling film/plastic wrap pierced with holes for the stems. Cook on HIGH for 3 minutes. Baste the pears with the cooking liquid, re-cover and cook a further 2 minutes on HIGH. Allow to cool completely. Remove the pears from the bowl. Place chocolate in a deep bowl and microwave on HIGH for 1½ minutes. Add 60ml/4 tbsps of the pear cooking liquid and stir well. Microwave on HIGH for 30 seconds. Stir to blend and fold in the cream. Cool completely and freeze the pears and the sauce separately. The pears may be frozen in a serving dish if desired. Cover both well. To thaw the pears, warm on LOW or DEFROST for 5 minutes and leave to stand for 10 minutes. Reheat for 1 minute on HIGH if desired, or serve cold. Defrost the sauce 2 minutes on LOW or DEFROST and leave to stand for 2 minutes. If desired, reheat the sauce for 1 minute on HIGH. Pour the sauce over the pears and garnish each pear with angelica cut into leaf shapes or with

**Facing page: Jamaican Mousse Cake.**

fresh mint leaves. Serve with whipped cream. Pears and sauce may be frozen for up to 3 weeks.

## Lemon-Lime Cheesecake

**PREPARATION TIME:** 25 minutes

**MICROWAVE COOKING TIME:** 2½ minutes plus standing time

**SERVES:** 6-8 people

*90g/3oz butter or margarine*
*180g/6oz digestive biscuits/graham crackers, finely crushed*
*450g/1lb cream cheese*
*120g/4oz/1 cup sugar*
*Grated rind and juice of 1 small lemon and 1 lime*
*3 eggs*
*15g/1 tbsp powdered gelatine*
*A few drops of green and yellow food colouring (optional)*

**GARNISH**
*140ml/¼ pint/½ cup whipped cream*
*Thin lemon and lime slices*

Place the butter in a small bowl and cook for 2 minutes on MEDIUM, or until melted. Stir in the crushed biscuits/crackers and press firmly into a lightly-greased loose-based dish and chill. Beat the cheese and sugar together until light and fluffy. Remove 30ml/2 tbsps of the juice to a small ramekin/custard cup and add the remaining juice and rind to the cheese and mix thoroughly. Sprinkle the gelatine on top of the reserved juice and leave to soak. Separate the eggs and beat the yolks gradually into the cheese mixture. Heat the gelatine for 30 seconds on HIGH and leave to stand for 2 minutes until clear. Pour the cleared gelatine into the cheese mixture and stir well. Whip the egg whites in a large bowl until they form stiff peaks, and fold into the cheese mixture. Pour the cheesecake mixture on top of the biscuit crust and chill until set. To freeze, remove the cheesecake from the dish but leave on the base. Freeze, uncovered, until firm and then wrap well. Freeze for up to 2 weeks. Best thawed overnight in the refrigerator or in a cool place for 2 hours. When defrosted, unwrap

the cheesecake and remove the base if metal. Place the cheesecake on a serving plate. Cook on HIGH for 2 minutes and then on LOW or DEFROST for 8 minutes. Leave to stand until completely defrosted. Decorate with rosettes of cream and thin slices of lemon and lime.

## Raspberry Yogurt Cake

**PREPARATION TIME:** 25 minutes plus chilling

**MICROWAVE COOKING TIME:** 4-6 minutes

**SERVES:** 6-8 people

This page: Lemon-Lime Cheesecake. Facing page: Raspberry Yogurt Cake.

**BASE**
*60g/4 tbsps butter or margarine*
*120g/4oz digestive biscuits/graham crackers, crushed*

**FILLING**
*15g/1 tbsp powdered gelatine*
*45ml/3 tbsps water*
*675g/1½ lbs raspberries*
*60g/4 tbsps sugar*
*280ml/½ pint/1 cup natural yogurt*
*15ml/1 tbsp raspberry liqueur or grenadine syrup*

# Chocolate-Raspberry Meringue Cake

**PREPARATION TIME:** 20 minutes

**MICROWAVE COOKING TIME:** 13-16 minutes

**SERVES:** 6-8 people

180g/6oz/1½ cups plain/all-purpose flour
7.5ml/1½ tsps bicarbonate of soda
60g/4 tbsps cocoa
225g/8oz/1 cup sugar
180g/6oz/⅔ cup butter or margarine
180ml/6 fl oz/¾ cup evaporated milk
15ml/1 tbsp white wine vinegar/distilled white vinegar
2 eggs, beaten
Few drops vanilla essence/extract
225g/8oz frozen raspberries
**TO FINISH**
3 egg whites
5ml/1 tsp cornflour/cornstarch
1.25ml/¼ tsp cream of tartar
90g/6 tbsps sugar
Toasted shredded/flaked coconut

Lightly grease a 2 litre/3 pint/6 cup cake ring. Sift the flour, soda and cocoa into a mixing bowl and add the sugar. Combine the evaporated milk and vinegar and set aside. Melt the butter or margarine on HIGH for 2-3 minutes or until liquid. Pour into the milk and vinegar and gradually add the beaten eggs. Pour into the dry ingredients and beat well. Pour into the cake ring and smooth down the top to level. Cook on HIGH for 10 minutes or until the top of the cake is only slightly sticky. Cool in the ring for 10 minutes then turn out onto a wire rack to cool completely. When cool cut in half around the middle and scoop out some of the crumbs on the top and bottom half to form a channel. Fill with the frozen raspberries, sandwich the cake together and cover it well. Freeze up to 2 months. Thaw the cake for 2 minutes on DEFROST and set aside. To prepare the meringue, place the egg whites, cornflour/cornstarch and cream of tartar in a mixing bowl. Beat until soft peaks form. Add the sugar, a spoonful at a time, continuing to beat until stiff peaks form. Spread the meringue over the

Heat the butter on HIGH for 2-3 minutes until melted. Stir in the crushed biscuits. Press onto the base of a loose-bottom dish and leave in the refrigerator to set. Sprinkle the gelatine over the water in a small bowl and leave to soak. Combine the raspberries and sugar in a large bowl and cook for 1-2 minutes on HIGH, stirring occasionally. Mash with a fork and then sieve out the seeds if desired. Warm the gelatine on HIGH for 1 minute until dissolved. Combine the yogurt with the raspberry purée and pour in the gelatine, stirring constantly. Add the liqueur or grenadine syrup and pour

**This page: Chocolate-Raspberry Meringue Cake. Facing page: White and Dark Chocolate Bombe.**

on top of the biscuit base and leave to set in the refrigerator. Freeze, remove from the dish but leave on the base. Freeze, unwrapped, until firm. Wrap well and return to the freezer for up to 1 month. Best thawed overnight in the refrigerator or in a cool place for about 2 hours. Alternatively, defrost as for Lemon-Lime Cheesecake. Garnish with rosettes of whipped cream and whole raspberries if desired.

cake and cover completely. Sprinkle on the toasted coconut and microwave on MEDIUM 3-6 minutes or until the meringue is set.

# White and Dark Chocolate Bombe

**PREPARATION TIME:** 30 minutes plus freezing

**MICROWAVE COOKING TIME:** 4½ minutes

**SERVES:** 6-8 people

*280ml/½ pint dark chocolate ice cream*
*10ml/2 tsps coffee powder*
*15ml/1 tbsp hot water*
*570ml/1 pint vanilla ice cream*
*120g/4oz white chocolate, broken up*
*60g/2oz ratafia/amaretti biscuits, coarsely crushed*

Place a 1150ml/2 pint/4 cup bombe mould or bowl into the freezer for 2 hours. Soften the dark chocolate ice cream on HIGH for 1 minute. Mix together the coffee powder and hot water in a small bowl and heat for 1 minute on HIGH. Stir into the chocolate ice cream. If the ice cream is too soft, freeze again until of spreading consistency. Coat the base and sides of the mould or bowl with the dark chocolate ice cream and freeze until firm. If the ice cream slides down the sides of the bowl during freezing, keep checking and pressing the ice cream back into place. Heat the vanilla ice cream on HIGH for 2 minutes or until very soft and almost liquid. Set aside and melt the white chocolate in a small bowl for 1 minute on HIGH or until soft. Fold the white chocolate into the vanilla ice cream and re-heat 2-3 minutes. Stir in the crushed biscuits. Freeze the ice cream until slushy and then pour into the centre of the dark chocolate ice cream, cover and freeze until solid. Half an hour before serving, unmould the bombe by briefly dipping in warm water or wrapping a hot cloth around the outside. Alternatively, if the mould is microwave-proof, heat for 30 seconds on HIGH and unmould. Decorate the top with grated plain/ semi-sweet or white chocolate.

# INDEX